SCHOLASTIC

2020
BOOK OF WORLD RECORDS

BY
CYNTHIA O'BRIEN
ABIGAIL MITCHELL
MICHAEL BRIGHT
DONALD SOMMERVILLE

Due to this book's publication date, the majority of statistics are current as of May 2019. The publisher does not have any control over and does not assume any responsibility for author or third-party websites or their content.

This book was created and produced by Toucan Books Limited.
Text: Michael Bright, Abigail Mitchell, Cynthia O'Brien, Donald Sommerville
Designer: Lee Riches
Editor: Anna Southgate
Proofreader: Richard Beatty
Index: Marie Lorimer
Toucan would like to thank Cian O'Day for picture research.

ISBN 978-1-338-57570-5

10 9 8 7 6 5 4 3 2 1   19 20 21 22 23

Printed in the U.S.A. 40

First printing, 2019

CONTENTS

MUSIC MAKERS

MUSIC MAKERS
TRENDING

"SWEET VICTORY"
Spongebob at the Super Bowl

The cartoon character Spongebob Squarepants left his pineapple under the sea to make his debut at Superbowl LIII. Before the show, more than 1.2 million people signed an online petition to allow a clip of Spongebob singing "Sweet Victory." The fans wanted to pay tribute to the cartoon's creator, Stephen Hillenburg, who died in November 2018. Spongebob and Squidward appeared in a short clip at halftime. After the show @SpongeBob tweeted "So honored and humbled! Thankful for being included."

HONORING HIP-HOP
Rap star gets Pulitzer

Kendrick Lamar broke records when he became the first rap musician to win the Pulitzer Prize. The Pulitzer Prize awards excellence in American literature, journalism, photography, poetry, and music. Until 1997, all the music winners were classical musicians. In that year, jazz musician Wynton Marsalis won the Pulitzer. Lamar, who won for his fourth studio album, was the first non-classical, non-jazz artist to win the prize.

BABY SHARK FEVER
Kiddie K-pop goes viral

It may be only ninety seconds long, but the video for Pinkfong's megahit, "Baby Shark," notched up over three billion YouTube views and topped the charts in several countries. The video borrows from the popular Korean-pop style, remixing it for preschool children. Its upbeat, sing-along tune and simple dance moves had kids streaming "Baby Shark" on repeat. The video also spurred a sing-along book featuring Baby Shark, Mama Shark, Daddy Shark, and Grandma Shark, complete with hand and foot movements for kids to mimic.

COACHELLA LIVESTREAMING
Tuning into Beyoncé

A record 458,000 people worldwide watched YouTube's livestream of Beyoncé's performance at Coachella in April 2018. For many, this meant watching very early in the morning or very late at night. Part of the draw was the highly anticipated reunion of Beyoncé's former all-girl group Destiny's Child. Also joining Queen Bey for parts of the almost two-hour set were her husband, Jay-Z, and her sister, Solange Knowles.

RINGING IN THE NUMBERS
Record views for new release

Ariana Grande's "7 rings" video became the biggest debut of 2019, with 23.6 million views in its first twenty-four hours on YouTube. The song also broke records on Spotify with 15 million streams in the first twenty-four hours and 71.4 million streams in its first week. Grande's record-breaking numbers continued with the release of her album, *thank u, next*. The album shot to no. 1 on the *Billboard* 200 and had the biggest streaming week for a pop album ever, with 307 million audio streams in its first week.

7

MOST-STREAMED song of 2018

"GOD'S PLAN"

With more than one billion plays on Spotify in 2018, Canadian rapper Drake took the crown for most-streamed song of 2018 with his hit "God's Plan." Apple also recognized the song as the most-streamed song on their Apple Music service. The song appears on the artist's album *Scorpion*, which was the most-streamed album of the year, and broke records as the first album to have one billion streams in its first week. That's up to ten million streams an hour! In this chart-topping year for Drake, he also became the platform's most-streamed artist of all time, with 8.2 billion streams in 2018 alone. His dominance in the music world was cemented with twelve top-ten songs over the year—more than even the Beatles had in their heyday.

MOST-STREAMED SONGS 2018

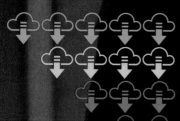

Drake: "God's Plan"

Post Malone (ft 21 Savage): "Rockstar"

Ed Sheeran: "Perfect"

Post Malone (ft Ty Dolla $ign): "Psycho"

Drake: "In My Feelings"

TOP-SELLING
album

REPUTATION
Taylor Swift

Taylor Swift's sixth studio album was released in November 2017, but still took the title of 2018's bestselling album. The pop star also became the first artist to have a bestselling album in three different years, having achieved the feat in 2014 with her '80s-inspired *1989* and in 2009 with country-pop album *Fearless*. *Reputation* saw Swift take on a darker persona than her earlier releases, and her video for the single "Look What You Made Me Do" famously saw her dressing up in costumes from the star's previous tours in an attempt to destroy her former self. This winning recipe led *Reputation* to sell 1.2 million copies in its first week; it was also the first album since Adele's *25* in 2015 to sell over two million copies (an achievement made by all of Swift's previous albums).

MOST-VIEWED online music video

"THANK U, NEXT"

Ariana Grande

Nickelodeon-actress-turned-popstar Ariana Grande paid tribute to her favorite romantic comedies in the music video for "thank u, next," breaking Vevo's all-time record for most-viewed music video in the first twenty-four hours. Her video, released in November 2018, had over fifty-five million views, and at one point had 829,000 people watching at once—also a record. "thank u, next" featured Grande and her friends reenacting scenes from movies such as *Legally Blonde* and *Mean Girls*, featuring celebrity cameos from actors and reality stars, such as Kris Jenner. "thank u, next" broke the previous record after twenty-two hours online.

TOP-EARNING tour ED SHEERAN

According to *Forbes*, British singer-songwriter Ed Sheeran had the top-earning tour of 2018 while touring for his album ÷ (*Divide*). The tour made $429,491,502 in 2018 alone, but also included tour dates in both 2017 and 2019. Sheeran's impressive 2018 title was no doubt helped by the fact that he played ninety-nine shows in 2018—fifty-one more than Taylor Swift, whose *Reputation* tour was the next highest earner in 2018 at $315 million. The ÷ tour began in Italy in March 2017 and ended in August 2019, and has been attended by over four million fans representing every continent. Sheeran had the most tour dates in Europe, where he played 117 shows, but also played eighteen gigs in Oceania and four in South Africa.

TOP-EARNING TOURS 2018
Revenue in millions of U.S. dollars

Ed Sheeran: 429

Taylor Swift: 315

Beyoncé and Jay-Z: 253

Bruno Mars: 237

Pink: 180

FIRST RAPPER TO TOP

Billboard 100 chart

DRAKE

Drake released his album *If You're Reading This It's Too Late* through iTunes on February 12, 2015. The digital album sold 495,000 units in its first week and entered the *Billboard* 100 at no. 1, making Drake the first rap artist ever to top the chart. The album also helped Drake secure another record: the most hits on the *Billboard* 100 at one time.

On March 7, 2015, Drake had fourteen hit songs on the chart, matching the record the Beatles have held since 1964. Since releasing his first hit single, "Best I Ever Had," in 2009, Drake has seen many of his singles go multiplatinum, including "Hotline Bling," which sold 41,000 copies in its first week and had eighteen weeks at no. 1 on the *Billboard* 100.

TOP GROUP/DUO
IMAGINE DRAGONS

TOP GROUP/DUOS 2018
1. Imagine Dragons
2. BTS
3. Migos
4. Maroon 5
5. Florida Georgia Line

Billboard named American rock band Imagine Dragons as the top group or duo of 2018 following a year of success. Early in 2018, the band broke records as the first artist to have three songs remain on the charts for a full calendar year with their song "Believer." Their hits "Radioactive" and "Demons," both from the album *Night Visions*, also sat on the Top 100 for more than fifty-two weeks.

Their 2017 album *Evolve* was monumentally successful in 2018, too, setting various records, including becoming the first work with three consecutive singles to hit number one on the charts. Imagine Dragons continued their prolific output with a new album, *Origins*, at the end of 2018. The band is made up of singer Dan Reynolds, guitarist Wayne Sermon, bassist Ben McKee, and drummer Daniel Platzman.

TOP-SELLING recording THE group
BEATLES

TOP-SELLING RECORDING GROUPS IN THE UNITED STATES
Albums sold in millions

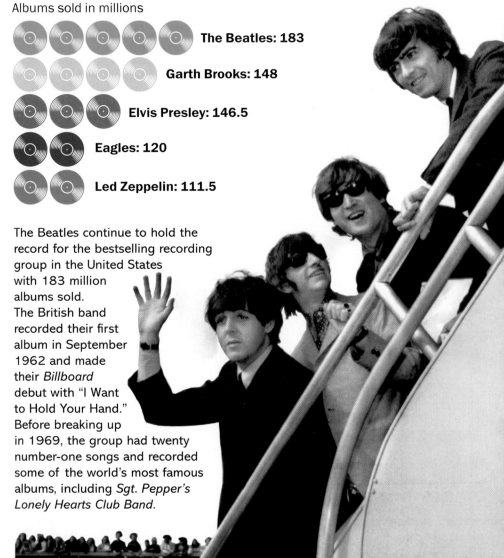

The Beatles: 183

Garth Brooks: 148

Elvis Presley: 146.5

Eagles: 120

Led Zeppelin: 111.5

The Beatles continue to hold the record for the bestselling recording group in the United States with 183 million albums sold. The British band recorded their first album in September 1962 and made their *Billboard* debut with "I Want to Hold Your Hand." Before breaking up in 1969, the group had twenty number-one songs and recorded some of the world's most famous albums, including *Sgt. Pepper's Lonely Hearts Club Band*.

SHORTEST CONCERT **ever** WHITE STRIPES

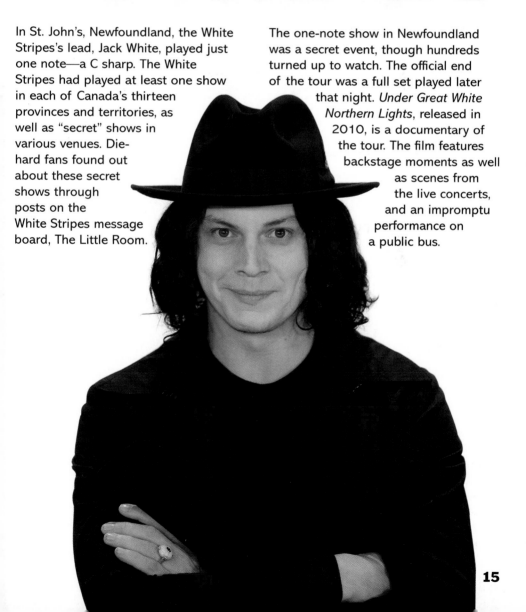

In St. John's, Newfoundland, the White Stripes's lead, Jack White, played just one note—a C sharp. The White Stripes had played at least one show in each of Canada's thirteen provinces and territories, as well as "secret" shows in various venues. Die-hard fans found out about these secret shows through posts on the White Stripes message board, The Little Room.

The one-note show in Newfoundland was a secret event, though hundreds turned up to watch. The official end of the tour was a full set played later that night. *Under Great White Northern Lights*, released in 2010, is a documentary of the tour. The film features backstage moments as well as scenes from the live concerts, and an impromptu performance on a public bus.

15

MOST-STREAMED
song ever
on Spotify

Ed Sheeran's "Shape of You" broke records in 2018 by becoming the first song to hit two billion streams on Spotify—a feat that also makes it the platform's most-streamed song ever. Originally written by Sheeran for Rihanna, the British singer-songwriter ended up releasing the song himself as part of his album ÷ (*Divide*), to massive success. "Shape of You" officially hit diamond status according to the Recording Industry Association of America in January 2019, meaning that it had achieved ten million units sold (or streaming sales equivalents). It also won Sheeran a Grammy award in 2018 for Best Pop Solo Performance.

"SHAPE
OF YOU"

ED SHEERAN

music video

"HAPPY"
BY PHARRELL

Pharrell Williams made history in November 2013 with the release of the first twenty-four-hour music video—the longest music video ever. The video for Williams's hit song "Happy" is a four-minute track that plays on a loop 360 times. In addition to Williams, celebrities such as Jamie Foxx, Steve Carell, and Miranda Cosgrove make appearances in the video. In 2014, "Happy" broke records again, becoming the first single to top six *Billboard* charts in one year and becoming the year's bestselling song with 6,455,000 digital copies sold.

TOP-EARNING
female
singer
KATY PERRY

American pop star Katy Perry was 2018's top-earning female singer, racking up $83 million before tax. This was not the first year for her to win the accolade, according to *Forbes*—she was also at the top of her game in 2015, when she earned an impressive $135 million in a single year. Although 2018's total is not quite as high, Perry's star is still bright. She played eighty tour dates in 2018, earning more than $1 million a night, and also counted on more than $20 million for her role as a judge on star-search show *American Idol*. The majority of her 2018 income came from these two sources—while her 2018 album *Witness* spent a week at number one, it was less well received than some of her previous efforts.

TOP-EARNING FEMALE SINGERS 2018
In millions of U.S. dollars

Katy Perry: 83
Taylor Swift: 80
Beyoncé: 60
Pink: 52
Lady Gaga: 50

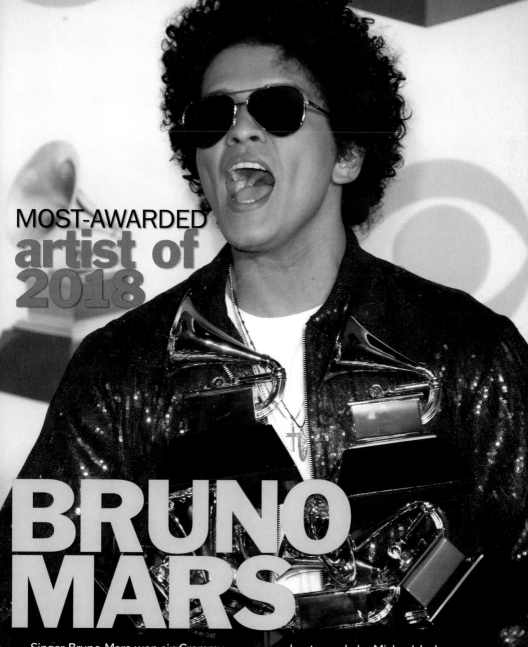

MOST-AWARDED
artist of
2018

BRUNO
MARS

Singer Bruno Mars won six Grammy Awards in 2018, including the coveted awards for song, record, and album of the year, for his 2017 album *24k Magic* and single "That's What I Like." His Grammy success put him at number three on the list of artists with the most Grammy wins in a single year, beaten only by Michael Jackson in 1984 and the rock band Santana in 2000, both of whom won eight awards in one night. Only nine artists in Grammy history have won six or more awards in one night, although British pop star Adele has achieved that feat twice.

ACT WITH THE MOST
Country Music
Awards
GEORGE STRAIT

"King of Country" George Strait won his first Country Music Award (CMA) in 1985 for Male Vocalist of the Year and Album of the Year. Since then, Strait has won an amazing twenty-three CMAs, including Entertainer of the Year in 2013. The country music superstar has thirty-three platinum or multiplatinum albums, and he holds the record for the most platinum certifications in country music. George Strait was inducted into the Country Music Hall of Fame in 2006.

MUSICIAN WITH THE MOST MTV Video Music Awards
BEYONCÉ

The queen of pop, Beyoncé, is the winningest VMA artist ever. She won eight MTV Video Music Awards in 2016 alone, pushing her ahead of Madonna's twenty VMA trophies and setting a new record of twenty-four VMA wins. The music video for "Formation," from Beyoncé's visual album *Lemonade*, won five awards, including the coveted prize for Video of the Year. With eight moon men from eleven nominations, Beyoncé tied the record for the most VMA wins in one year by a female solo artist, also held by Lady Gaga.

MUSICIAN WITH THE MOST MTV VIDEO MUSIC AWARDS

Beyoncé: 24

Madonna: 20

Lady Gaga: 13

Peter Gabriel: 13

Eminem: 12

TOP country song "MEANT TO BE"

TOP COUNTRY SONGS 2017–2018
Number of weeks at no. 1 on Hot Country Songs

♫ ♫ ♫ ♫ ♫ **Bebe Rexha and Florida Georgia Line "Meant to Be": 50**

♫ ♫ ♫ ♫ **Sam Hunt, "Body Like a Back Road": 34**

♫ ♫ ♫ **Florida Georgia Line, "Cruise": 25**

♫ ♫ **Leroy Van Dyke, "Walk On By": 19**

♫ **Florida Georgia Line, "H.O.L.Y.": 18**

The collaboration between American country duo Florida Georgia Line and pop star Bebe Rexha broke an all-time record for sitting at the top of *Billboard*'s Hot Country Songs for fifty weeks. The year 2018 was not the first in which the duo, consisting of singers Tyler Hubbard and Brian Kelley, has topped the country song chart—in 2012, their song "Cruise" stayed at number one for six consecutive months. "Meant to Be" came about as a result of a last-minute writing session between Rexha and Florida Georgia Line in Nashville, Tennessee, after pop singer Charlie Puth pulled out of a scheduled meeting. Rexha claims to have mistaken Florida Georgia Line for another country group before they sat down to write, but this did not stop the trio from writing one of the year's most popular crossover songs.

MOST-PLAYED
rock song 2018:
"BROKEN"

Indie trio lovelytheband's breakthrough hit "broken" successfully propelled them into the alternative scene, spending nine weeks at number one on the *Billboard* Alternative Songs airplay chart. The first single from the group's debut album *finding it hard to smile*, "broken" was cowritten by band members Mitchy Collins, Jordan Greenwald, and Sam Price. By the end of 2018, "broken" was on track to compete for the longest run of any song on the Alternative airplay chart at fifty-five weeks. On March 2, 2019, it officially broke the record for the longest-running alternative song with sixty-six weeks on the chart, beating out former leaders, Rise Against. Their hit "Savior" had spent sixty-five weeks on the Alternative chart in 2009–10.

ROCK SONGS WITH MOST AIRPLAY 2018
1. lovelytheband: "broken"
2. Foster the People: "Sit Next to Me"
3. Imagine Dragons: "Whatever it Takes"
4. Portugal. The Man: "Live in the Moment"
5. Imagine Dragons: "Natural"

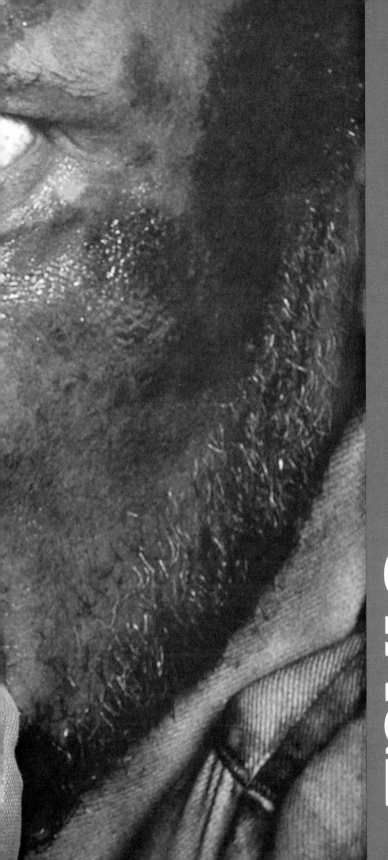

screen &
STAGE

SCREEN & STAGE
TRENDING#↑

SUPERHERO CAREER
Wolverine actor goes the distance

Hugh Jackman has set the record for having the longest career playing a live-action Marvel superhero. Jackman began playing the character Wolverine in 2000 when he starred in the first *X-Men* movie. Altogether, Jackman played the role for 16 years and 228 days. Jackman shared the award with his costar, Sir Patrick Stewart, who played Professor X for the same number of years.

NETFLIX AT THE OSCARS
Nomination for streaming giant

For the first time, streaming giant Netflix won a best picture Oscar nomination in 2018. The film, *Roma*, also won nominations in nine other categories, including a Best Director nod for Alfonso Cuarón. *Roma* went on to win three Oscars for Best Director, Best Cinematography, and Best Foreign Language Film. A win in this last category was a first for Mexico.

HOT TICKET
Cinemas reopen in Saudi Arabia

In April 2018, Saudi Arabia opened its first cinema in thirty-five years with a screening of *Black Panther*. The government, encouraged by religious leaders, banned and closed theaters across the country in 1983. The reboot of cinema culture began with a private showing of *Black Panther* in a concert hall in the country's capital, Riyadh, followed by public screenings. Saudi Arabia expects to have 350 theaters and 2,500 screens operating by 2030.

ROYAL ROMANCE
Harry and Meghan tie the knot

A record-breaking, near-thirty million Americans tuned in to watch the wedding of Britain's Prince Harry and retired American actress Meghan Markle on May 19, 2018. By contrast, twenty-three million Americans watched the wedding of Harry's brother, Prince William, and Kate Middleton in 2011.

FANTASTIC FASHION
Red-carpet look stuns

Ezra Miller set the Internet on fire after his red-carpet appearance in Paris for the movie premiere of *Fantastic Beasts: The Crimes of Grindelwald*. The cause of the stir was Miller's outfit, a hooded, floor-length, puffer-jacket and dress combo. Pierpaolo Piccioli, the creative director for fashion house Valentino, worked with Italian sportswear company, Moncler, to create the look for the company's Genius collection.

27

LONGEST-RUNNING
scripted TV show in the United States THE SIMPSONS

MATT GROENING

In 2018, *The Simpsons* entered a record thirtieth season, making it the longest-running American sitcom, cartoon, and scripted prime-time television show in history. The animated comedy, which first aired in December 1989, centers on the antics and everyday lives of the Simpson family. The show's creator, Matt Groening, named the characters after members of his own family, although he substituted Bart for his own name. In 2018, the show's guest stars included Ed Sheeran and Gal Gadot.

TV SHOW WITH THE MOST Emmy Awards

SATURDAY NIGHT LIVE

The variety show *Saturday Night Live* won eight Emmy Awards in 2018, including the award for Outstanding Variety Sketch Series. The late-night comedy show broadcasts live from New York City's Rockefeller Center on Saturday nights. A new celebrity host introduces the show each week and takes part in comedy skits with the regular cast. *Saturday Night Live* launched the careers of many of America's top comedians, including Will Ferrell, Tina Fey, and Kristen Wiig, many of whom return to the show regularly in guest spots. In the awards of 2018, Outstanding Guest Actress in a Comedy Series went to Tiffany Haddish for her stint as the show's host in November 2017. The event marked the first time in the show's history for a black female stand-up comic to take up the hosting spot.

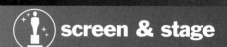

HIGHEST-PAID
TV
actress SOFÍA
VERGARA

For the third year running, *Modern Family*'s Sofía Vergara holds top spot for the highest-paid actress on television in 2018, earning $42.5 million. While much of Vergara's income is down to her role as Gloria Delgado-Pritchett in *Modern Family*, almost half of it comes from endorsements and licensing deals that include coffee maker SharkNinja Coffee and furniture chain Rooms To Go. Vergara, who is originally from Colombia, has won four Screen Actors Guild Awards as part of the *Modern Family* cast for Outstanding Performance by an Ensemble in a Comedy Series.

TOP-EARNING TV ACTRESSES
In millions of U.S. dollars

Sofía Vergara: 42.5

Kaley Cuoco: 24.5

Ellen Pompeo: 23.5

Mariska Hargitay: 13

Julie Bowen: 12.5

ON MY BLOCK

MOST-BINGED
original Netflix
show of 2018

MOST-BINGED ORIGINAL NETFLIX SHOWS OF 2018

1. *On My Block*
2. *Making a Murderer: Part Two*
3. *13 Reasons Why: Season 2*
4. *Last Chance U: INDY*
5. *Bodyguard*

While TV streaming platform Netflix is notorious for keeping viewing figures under wraps, it did reveal its most binge-watched original programming for 2018. Taking the top spot was *On My Block*, a ten-episode series that debuted with little fanfare on March 16. *On My Block* is a teen comedy drama starring a diverse cast of newcomers—Jason Genao, Sierra Capri, Diego Tinoco, and Brett Gray—as a group of fourteen-year-old friends living in a gang-ruled Los Angeles neighborhood. The coming-of-age story earned an impressive 95 percent rating on *Rotten Tomatoes* for its freshman season, as well as plenty of online speculation over its cliffhanger finale.

MOST-WATCHED
television
broadcast of 2018
SUPER BOWL LII

The most-watched television broadcast of 2018 was Super Bowl LII, which saw forty-three million viewers between the ages of eighteen and forty-nine tune in to watch the Philadelphia Eagles beat the New England Patriots 31–33 on February 4. It was the Eagles' first-ever win of the prestigious trophy. The Super Bowl's accolade comes as no surprise, with NFL shows making up thirty-three of the one hundred most-watched TV broadcasts in the United States.

Jim Parsons was yet again TV's highest-paid actor in 2018, earning $26.5 million. Most of his income came from playing television's favorite physicist, Sheldon Cooper, in *The Big Bang Theory*. His costars Johnny Galecki, Simon Helberg, and Kunal Nayyar also made the top five—unsurprising, given that the sitcom was the third-most-watched show of the 2017–2018 season. Parsons appeared in numerous TV shows before getting his big break in 2006 with a lead role as Sheldon. He has since won four Emmy Awards for Outstanding Lead Actor in a Comedy Series.

HIGHEST-PAID
TV actor JIM
PARSONS

HIGHEST-PAID TV ACTORS
In millions of U.S. dollars

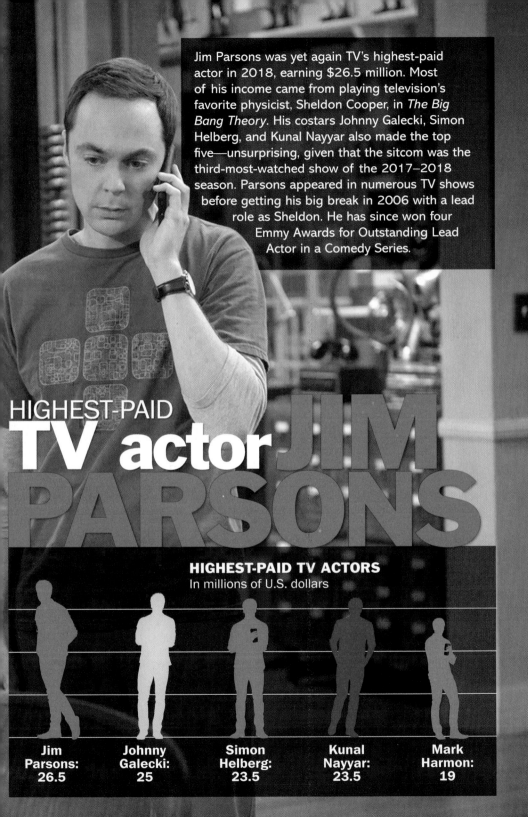

| Jim Parsons: 26.5 | Johnny Galecki: 25 | Simon Helberg: 23.5 | Kunal Nayyar: 23.5 | Mark Harmon: 19 |

MOVIE WITH THE HIGHEST production costs

MOVIES WITH THE HIGHEST PRODUCTION COSTS
In millions of U.S. dollars

Pirates of the Caribbean: On Stranger Tides: 378.5

Avengers: Age of Ultron: 365.5

Avengers: Infinity War: 316

Pirates of the Caribbean: At World's End: 300

Justice League: 300

Pirates of the Caribbean: On Stranger Tides cost a huge $378.5 million to produce, almost $80 million more than *Pirates of the Caribbean: At World's End*, released four years earlier. The 2011 movie was the fourth in Walt Disney's Pirates of the Caribbean franchise starring Johnny Depp as Captain Jack Sparrow. In this installment of the wildly popular series, Captain Jack goes in search of the Fountain of Youth. Depp earned $55.5 million for the role, and the movie went on to earn $1.04 billion worldwide. In 2017, Johnny Depp returned to play Captain Jack in *Pirates of the Caribbean: Dead Men Tell No Tales*, the latest title in the franchise.

PIRATES OF THE CARIBBEAN
ON STRANGER TIDES

MOST
SUCCESSFUL
movie franchise
MARVEL CINEMATIC UNIVERSE

The Marvel Comics superhero movie franchise has grossed more than $17.45 billion worldwide—and counting! This impressive total includes ticket sales from the huge hits of 2018, *Black Panther* and *Avengers: Infinity War*. *Black Panther* grossed $1.34 billion worldwide within three months of its release, but then *Avengers: Infinity War* hit the screens, taking $1.82 billion worldwide in its first month. With *Avengers: Endgame* earning even greater revenues in 2019, Marvel Cinematic Universe looks set to hold this record for the foreseeable future.

Marvel Cinematic Universe: 17.45

Star Wars: 9.29

Harry Potter: 9.05

James Bond: 7.04

Middle Earth: 5.88

MOST SUCCESSFUL MOVIE FRANCHISES
Total worldwide gross, in billions of U.S. dollars, as of March 2019

movies with the most
OSCARS

MOVIES WITH THE MOST OSCARS

Ben-Hur (1959): 11

Titanic (1997): 11

The Lord of the Rings: The Return of the King (2003): 11

West Side Story (1961): 10

Gigi (1958); *The Last Emperor* (1987); *The English Patient* (1996): 9

It's a three-way tie for the movie with the most Academy Awards: *Ben-Hur*, *Titanic*, and *The Lord of the Rings: The Return of the King* have each won eleven Oscars, including Best Picture and Best Director. The 1959 biblical epic *Ben-Hur* was the first to achieve this record number of wins. *Titanic*, based on the real 1912 disaster, won numerous Oscars for its striking visual and sound effects. *The Lord of the Rings: The Return of the King* was the third in a trilogy based on the books by J. R. R. Tolkien. It is the only movie of the top three to win in every category in which it was nominated.

WHO'S OSCAR?

Every year the Academy of Motion Picture Arts and Sciences presents awards in recognition of the greatest achievements in the film industry. Those actors, directors, screenwriters, and producers lucky enough to win each receive a highly prized golden statuette, aka "Oscar." No one really knows where the name comes from, although it is thought to have originated among the Hollywood greats of the 1930s—Bette Davis and Walt Disney have been credited, among others. Either way, "Oscar" became the official nickname for the Academy Award in 1939.

YOUNGEST ACTRESS nominated for an Oscar

QUVENZHANÉ WALLIS

At nine years old, Quvenzhané Wallis became the youngest-ever Academy Award nominee. The actress received the Best Actress nomination in 2013 for her role as Hushpuppy in *Beasts of the Southern Wild*. Although Wallis did not win the Oscar, she went on to gain forty-one more nominations and win twenty-four awards at various industry award shows. In 2015, she received a Golden Globe Best Actress nomination for her role in *Annie*. Wallis was five years old when she auditioned for Hushpuppy (the minimum age was six), and she won the part over four thousand other candidates.

Justin Henry was just seven years old when he received a Best Supporting Actor nomination for *Kramer vs. Kramer* in 1980. His neighbor, a casting director, suggested that Henry try out for the part. Although the young actor lost out on the Oscar, *Kramer vs. Kramer* won several Oscars, including Best Actor for Dustin Hoffman, Best Actress in a Supporting Role for Meryl Streep, and Best Picture. Justin Henry appeared in a few other films before leaving acting to finish his education. He then returned to acting in the 1990s.

YOUNGEST ACTOR
nominated for an Oscar
JUSTIN HENRY

MOVIE WITH THE
MOST SUCCESSFUL
domestic opening
weekend

AVENGERS:
ENDGAME

WORLDWIDE *AVENGERS* OPENING WEEKENDS:

$1.2 billion
AVENGERS: ENDGAME (2019)

$640.5 million
AVENGERS: INFINITY WAR (2018)

$392.5 million
AVENGERS: AGE OF ULTRON (2015)

Avengers: Endgame broke the record set by *Avengers: Infinity War* to become the movie with the most successful opening weekend ever in the United States. On its release in April 2019, *Endgame* took an astonishing $357 million in its opening weekend in the United States. *Infinity War*, its chronological Marvel Cinematic Universe (MCU) predecessor, took home $257.6 on its own opening weekend—an impressive number, even if it was nearly $100 million less than *Endgame*. *Endgame* made box-office history with a record-breaking $1.2 billion sales worldwide in its opening run. It represents the finale to phase three of the MCU series, which at the time encompassed twenty-two movies.

ACTRESSES WITH THE MOST
MTV Movie Awards
JENNIFER LAWRENCE AND KRISTEN STEWART

ACTRESSES WITH THE MOST MTV MOVIE AWARDS

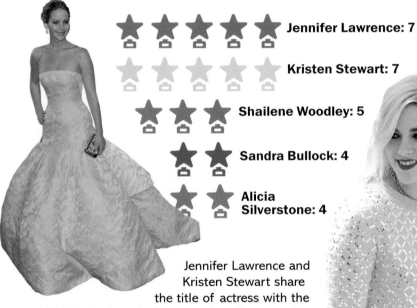

★ ★ ★ ★ ★ **Jennifer Lawrence: 7**

★ ★ ★ ★ ★ **Kristen Stewart: 7**

★ ★ ★ **Shailene Woodley: 5**

★ ★ **Sandra Bullock: 4**

★ ★ **Alicia Silverstone: 4**

Jennifer Lawrence and Kristen Stewart share the title of actress with the most MTV Movie Awards. Stewart won all seven of her awards for her role as Bella Swan in the movie adaptations of the Twilight franchise—including four Best Kiss awards with costar Robert Pattinson. Lawrence's seventh award was for Best Hero, which she won in 2016 for her role as Katniss Everdeen in the fourth installment of the popular Hunger Games franchise. The actress, however, was a no-show at the awards ceremony that year, due to press commitments for her upcoming movie *X-Men: Apocalypse*.

ACTOR WITH THE MOST

JIM
MTV Movie Awards
CARREY

Jim Carrey has eleven MTV Movie Awards, including five Best Comedic Performance awards for his roles in *Dumb and Dumber* (1994), *Ace Ventura: When Nature Calls* (1995), *The Cable Guy* (1996), *Liar Liar* (1997), and *Yes Man* (2008). He won the Best Villain award twice, once for *The Cable Guy* (1996) and the second time for *Dr. Seuss' How the Grinch Stole Christmas* (2000). Fans also awarded Carrey with the Best Kiss award for his lip-lock with Lauren Holly in *Dumb and Dumber*.

ACTORS WITH THE MOST MTV MOVIE AWARDS

★★★★★ Jim Carrey: 11

★★★★ Robert Pattinson: 10

★★★ Mike Myers: 7

★★ Adam Sandler: 6

★★ Will Smith: 6

SCARLETT JOHANSSON

TOP-EARNING actress

The highest-paid actress of 2018 was Scarlett Johansson, who earned $40.5 million before tax. This quadrupled her earnings from the previous year, largely thanks to the increasingly high paydays for movies within the expanding Marvel Cinematic Universe. Johansson plays the Black Widow Natasha Romanov in the superhero franchise. Johansson is not the only superhero to make the top ten earnings list. Gal Gadot, who plays DC's Wonder Woman, came tenth on the list with $10 million, and Cate Blanchett, eighth on the list with $12.5 million, portrayed underworld goddess Hela in Marvel's *Thor: Ragnarok*.

TOP-EARNING ACTRESSES OF 2018
In millions of U.S. dollars

Scarlett Johansson: 40.5

Angelina Jolie: 28

Jennifer Aniston: 19.5

Jennifer Lawrence: 18

Reese Witherspoon: 16.5

44

TOP-EARNING
actor
THE ROCK

According to *Forbes*, Dwayne "The Rock" Johnson earned a cool $124 million pretax in 2018, almost doubling his $64.5 million of 2017. The increase is down to the star's huge social following, which enables financial deals outside of his acting career. George Clooney earned almost twice as much in 2018, after selling his whiskey label, but The Rock earned the most from acting—and more than any actor has earned from acting in the history of *Forbes*'s Celebrity 100 list. A large chunk of Johnson's income came from the making of *Jumanji: Welcome to the Jungle*.

TOP-EARNING ACTORS OF 2018
In millions of U.S. dollars

The Rock: 124

Robert Downey Jr.: 81

Chris Hemsworth: 64.5

Jackie Chan: 45.5

Will Smith: 42

TOP-GROSSING movie BLACK PANTHER

Four top-grossing movies made 2018 a blockbuster year for superheroes. The most successful was Marvel's *Black Panther*, which earned over $700 million in the United States. Without taking inflation into account, its worldwide gross total exceeded that of *Titanic*, and *Black Panther* became the tenth movie to gross over $1.3 billion worldwide. Set in the fictional technological utopia of Wakanda, *Black Panther* stars a majority-black cast headed by Chadwick Boseman as T'Challa, the titular hero. The movie's famous "Wakanda Forever" salute has also taken on a life outside of the story, going viral on social media and even being echoed by black athletes during sporting events.

TOP-EARNING MOVIES 2018
Gross in millions of U.S. dollars

Black Panther:
700.06

Avengers: Infinity War: 678.82

Incredibles 2: 608.58

Jurassic World: Fallen Kingdom: 417.72

Aquaman: 335

TOP-GROSSING
animated-film
franchise

DESPICABLE ME

Following the hugely successful 2017 release of the third movie in the series, *Despicable Me 3*, and with a global total of $3.528 billion, Despicable Me became the world's highest-grossing animated franchise of all time. The 2015 spin-off *Minions* is the most profitable animated film in Universal Studios' history and was the highest-grossing film of the year, while *Despicable Me 3* and Oscar-nominated *Despicable Me 2* hit spot no. 2 in their respective years of release. Collectively the four movies beat the Shrek franchise's takings of $3.51 billion, a total that includes sales from the spin-off *Puss in Boots*.

Andrew Lloyd Webber's *The Phantom of the Opera* opened on Broadway in January 1988 and has been performed more than 13,000 times. The original London cast members Michael Crawford, Sarah Brightman, and Steve Barton reprised their roles on Broadway. The story, based on a novel written in 1911 by French author Gaston Leroux, tells the tragic tale of the phantom and his love for an opera singer, Christine.

LONGEST-RUNNING
Broadway show
THE PHANTOM OF THE OPERA

LONGEST-RUNNING BROADWAY SHOWS
Total performances (as of May 2019)

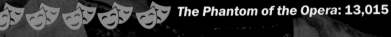

The Phantom of the Opera: 13,015

Chicago (1996 revival): 9,339

The Lion King: 8,945

Cats: 7,485

Les Misérables: 6,680

HIGHEST-GROSSING
Broadway musical
THE LION KING

Since opening on November 13, 1997, *The Lion King* has earned $1.6 billion. The show is Broadway's third-longest-running production. *The Lion King* stage show is an adaptation of the hugely popular Disney animated film. Along with hit songs from the movie such as "Circle of Life" and "Hakuna Matata," the show includes new compositions by South African composer Lebo M. and others. The Broadway show features songs in six African languages, including Swahili and Congolese. Since it opened, *The Lion King* has attracted audiences totaling over eighty million people.

MUSICAL WITH THE MOST Tony Award nominations
HAMILTON

Lin-Manuel Miranda's musical biography of Founding Father Alexander Hamilton racked up an amazing sixteen Tony Award nominations to unseat the previous record holders, *The Producers* and *Billy Elliot the Musical*, both of which had fifteen. The mega-hit hip-hop musical, which was inspired by historian Ron Chernow's biography of the first secretary of the treasury, portrays the Founding Fathers of the United States engaging in rap battles over issues such as the national debt and the French Revolution. *Hamilton* won eleven Tonys at the 2016 ceremony—one shy of *The Producers*, which retains the record for most Tony wins with twelve. *Hamilton*'s Broadway success paved the way for the show to open in Chicago in 2016, with a touring show and a London production following in 2017.

YOUNGEST WINNER
of a Laurence Olivier Award

In 2012, four actresses shared an Olivier Award for their roles in the British production of *Matilda*. Eleanor Worthington-Cox, Cleo Demetriou, Kerry Ingram, and Sophia Kiely all won the award for Best Actress in a Musical. Of the four actresses, Worthington-Cox, age ten, was the youngest by a few weeks. Each actress portraying Matilda performs two shows a week. In the U.S., the four *Matilda* actresses won a special Tony Honors for Excellence in the Theatre in 2013. *Matilda*, inspired by the book by Roald Dahl, won a record seven Olivier Awards in 2012.

ELEANOR WORTHINGTON-COX

CLEO DEMETRIOU

KERRY INGRAM

SOPHIA KIELY

on the
MOVE

ON THE MOVE
TRENDING#

NEW KIDS ON THE BLOCK
Best inventions of 2018

A life-saving drone and an electric semi-truck were among *Time* magazine's choices for the best fifty inventions of 2018. The lifesaving drone carries medical supplies quickly to remote areas. The electric semi-truck may replace fuel-burning trucks. Among other inventions on the list were a magic wand that teaches coding and a flying suit with mini jet engines.

REACH FOR A STAR
NASA's probe headed to the Sun

NASA's Parker Solar Probe rocketed into space in August 2018 and into the record books. The probe will zoom up to 430,000 miles per hour and travel to within 3.8 million miles of the Sun. This is much faster and more than seven times closer to the Sun than any probe has come before. During the seven-year mission, the probe will orbit the Sun twenty-four times and study its corona, the outer part of the Sun's atmosphere.

TEN MILLION MUSTANGS
Car company marked a milestone

Ford celebrated the making of its ten-millionth Mustang. The company first displayed the vehicle at New York's 1964 World's Fair and has sold Mustangs ever since. The first one ever purchased was a blue convertible by Gail Wise, who bought the convertible for just under $3,500. Today, her Mustang is worth as much as $450,000. Ford put the old and new car on display as part of their celebrations.

UP, UP, AND AWAY
Green light for world's longest aircraft

Airlander 10 got approval to go to full production. British company Hybrid Air Vehicles built the 302-foot-long hybrid aircraft that uses helium and four powerful diesel engines to fly. The eco-friendly aircraft uses much less fuel than a traditional airplane. Once in service, the aircraft will be able to take nineteen travelers on luxury flights.

SPACE TOURISM
Spacecraft for amateur astronauts

The Virgin Galactic spacecraft traveled to the edge of space in December 2018, flying over fifty miles above the earth. The flight began with a lift from a special jet that carried the spacecraft about 50,000 feet into the air. At that point, the spacecraft detached and rocketed up. The successful test flight was a big win for Virgin. The company plans to bring paying passengers into space in the future. More than 600 people have already bought tickets.

WORLD'S first MONSTER SCHOOL BUS

"Bad to the Bone" is the first monster school bus in the world. This revamped 1956 yellow bus is 13 feet tall, thanks to massive tires with 25-inch rims. The oversize bus weighs 19,000 pounds and is a favorite ride at charity events in California. But don't expect to get anywhere in a hurry—this "Kool Bus" is not built for speed and goes at a maximum of just 7 miles per hour.

MOST EXPENSIVE
street-legal car
LA VOITURE NOIRE

In February 2019, La Voiture Noire (The Black Car) claimed the crown as the world's most expensive car after being sold for $12.5 million. Only one of these cars was produced by luxury French supercar maker Bugatti, in celebration of its 110th anniversary. Said to take inspiration from the manufacturer's Type 57 SC Atlantic of the 1930s, as well as Darth Vader from *Star Wars*, the car features a sleek, all-black design with six tail pipes. At top speed, this exclusive vehicle can hit 261 miles per hour and can reach 62 miles per hour in 2.4 seconds.

MOST EXPENSIVE CARS
(as of 2019) In U.S. dollars

$$$$$

$$$$$

$$$$

Bugatti La Voiture Noire:
$12.5 million

Rolls-Royce Sweptail:
$10.5 million

Koenigsegg CCXR Trevita:
$4.8 million

$$$$

$$$

Lamborghini Veneno:
$4.5 million

McLaren P1M:
$3.6 million

WORLD'S BIGGEST
monster
truck
BIGFOOT 5

Standing 15 feet 6 inches tall and weighing 38,000 pounds, Bigfoot #5 is the king of monster trucks. Bob Chandler purchased a Ford pickup truck in 1974 and began creating the first Bigfoot monster truck in 1975. In 1986, Chandler introduced Bigfoot #5, the largest ever. The truck's tires are 10 feet tall and come from an Alaskan land train used by the U.S. Army in the 1950s. Chandler built over a dozen more Bigfoot trucks, but none of these newbies matches the size of Bigfoot #5.

WORLD'S SMALLEST trailer
QTVAN

The tiny QTvan is just over 7 feet long, 2.5 feet wide, and 5 feet tall. Inside, however, it has a full-size single bed, a kettle for boiling water, and a 19-inch TV. The Environmental Transport Association (ETA) in Britain sponsored the invention of the minitrailer, which was designed to be pulled by a mobility scooter. The ETA recommends the QTvan for short trips only, since mobility scooters have a top speed of 6 miles per hour, at best.

FASTEST land vehicle THRUST SSC

The world's fastest car is the Thrust SSC, which reached a speed of 763 miles per hour on October 15, 1997, in the Black Rock Desert, Nevada. *SSC* stands for supersonic (faster than the speed of sound). The Thrust SSC's amazing speed comes from two jet engines with 110,000 brake horsepower. That's as much as 145 Formula One race cars. The British-made car uses about 5 gallons of jet fuel in one second and takes just five seconds to reach its top speed. At that speed, the Thrust SSC could travel from New York City to San Francisco in less than four hours. More recently, another British manufacturer has developed a new supersonic car, the Bloodhound, with a projected speed of 1,000 miles per hour. If it reaches that, it will set a new world record.

FASTEST
passenger train
SHANGHAI
MAGLEV

The Shanghai Maglev, which runs between Shanghai Pudong International Airport and the outskirts of Shanghai, is the fastest passenger train in the world. The service reaches speeds of up to 267 miles per hour, covering the 19-mile distance in seven and a half minutes. "Maglev" is short for magnetic levitation, as the train moves by floating on magnets rather than with wheels on a track. Other high-speed trains, such as Japan's SCMaglev, may have reached higher speeds in testing (375 miles per hour), but are capped at 200 miles per hour when carrying passengers.

FASTEST PASSENGER TRAINS
(maximum operating speed)

Shanghai Maglev:
267 mph

China Fuxing Hao:
249 mph

Japan Shinkansen:
224 mph

Italy Italo:
220 mph

Italy Frecciarossa:
220 mph

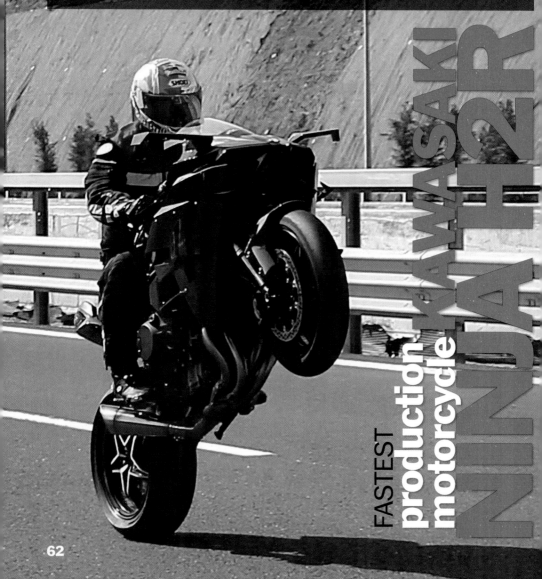

In June 2016, World Supersport rider Kenan Sofuoğlu set a new land-speed record for a production motorcycle—that is, a mass-produced, road-worthy, two-wheeled motorcycle. He reached a top speed of 249 miles per hour in just twenty-six seconds. He was riding the Kawasaki Ninja H2R, currently the fastest production motorcycle in the world, while crossing the Osman Gazi Bridge in Turkey. At 8,799 feet across, this is the world's fourth-longest suspension bridge. The Ninja H2R is currently legal for track racing only, and while Kawasaki produces a street-legal Ninja, it is not the world's fastest. That honor goes to the Madmax Streetfighter, which has a top speed of 233 miles per hour.

FASTEST production motorcycle

KAWASAKI NINJA H2R

LARGEST cruise ship ROYAL CARIBBEAN
Symphony of the Seas

SYMPHONY of the SEAS

With a gross tonnage of 230,000 tons, the new Royal Caribbean cruise ship *Symphony of the Seas* now holds the record for the world's largest. It beats last year's record holder, the 226,963-GT *Harmony of the Seas*, also a Royal Caribbean ship. *Symphony of the Seas* has 2,774 cabins and can carry 5,535 guests at full capacity. The two-story Ultimate Family Suite has an air-hockey table, a LEGO® climbing wall, and a private 3-D movie room with a library of video games and its own popcorn machine.

WORLD'S LARGEST CRUISE SHIPS
Gross tonnage (in tons)

 *Symphony of the Seas,* **Royal Caribbean: 230,000**

 *Harmony of the Seas,* **Royal Caribbean: 226,963**

 *Allure of the Seas,* **Royal Caribbean: 225,282**

 *Oasis of the Seas,* **Royal Caribbean: 225,282**

 *AIDANova:* **184,000**

on the move

FASTEST
helicopter circumnavigation of Earth

JENNIFER MURRAY AND COLIN BODILL

In 2007, British pilots Jennifer Murray and Colin Bodill became the first pilots ever to fly around the world in a helicopter via the North and South Poles. They also set the record for the fastest time to complete this journey, at 170 days, 22 hours, 47 minutes, and 17 seconds. The pair began and ended their record-setting journey in Fort Worth, Texas, and flew a Bell 407 helicopter. The journey, which began on December 5, 2006, and ended on May 23, 2007, was the duo's second attempt at the record. The first, in 2003, ended with an emergency rescue after they crashed in Antarctica.

LIGHTEST jet BD-5J MICROJET

In 2004, the BD-5J Microjet, a one-seater aircraft, secured the record as the world's lightest jet. The jet weighs 358.8 pounds, has a 17-foot wingspan, and is only 12 feet long. Engineer Jim Bede introduced the microjet in the early 1970s and sold hundreds in kit form, ready for self-assembly. The BD-5J model became a popular airshow attraction and was featured in a James Bond movie. The microjet uses a TRS-18 turbojet engine and can carry only 32 gallons of fuel. Its top speed is 300 miles per hour.

65

FASTEST unmanned plane X-43A

In November 2004, NASA launched its experimental X-43A plane for a test flight over the Pacific Ocean. The X-43A plane reached Mach 9.6, which is more than nine times the speed of sound and nearly 7,000 miles per hour. A B-52B aircraft carried the X-43A and a Pegasus rocket booster into the air, releasing them at 40,000 feet. At that point, the booster—essentially a fuel-packed engine—ignited, blasting the unmanned X-43A higher and faster, before separating from the plane. The plane continued to fly for several minutes at 110,000 feet, before crashing (intentionally) into the ocean.

FASTEST
man-made object

PARKER SOLAR PROBE

On October 29, 2018, the Parker Solar Probe broke a record that had not been beaten since 1976. Traveling at 155,959 miles per hour, it became the fastest man-made object ever known. Jointly operated by NASA and the Johns Hopkins University, and equipped with a wide range of scientific equipment, the Parker Solar Probe was on a mission to travel as close to the Sun as possible. The day after breaking the speed record, the probe had reached a distance of 25,072,700 miles from the Sun's surface—the closest a spacecraft has ever been. Withstanding extreme heat and radiation, the probe will study the Sun's atmosphere, sending data and images back to Earth, revolutionizing our understanding of the star at the heart of our solar system.

APOLLO 10 FLIGHT STATS

05/18/69
LAUNCH DATE: May 18, 1969

12:49
LAUNCH TIME: 12:49 p.m. EDT

05/21/69
ENTERED LUNAR ORBIT: May 21, 1969

192:03:23
DURATION OF MISSION: 192 hours, 3 minutes, 23 seconds

05/26/69
RETURN DATE: May 26, 1969

12:52
SPLASHDOWN: 12:52 p.m. EDT

FASTEST
manned
spacecraft
APOLLO 10

NASA's Apollo 10 spacecraft reached its top speed on its descent to Earth, hurtling through the atmosphere at 24,816 miles per hour and splashing down on May 26, 1969. The spacecraft's crew had traveled faster than anyone on Earth. The mission was a "dress rehearsal" for the first moon landing by Apollo 11, two months later. The Apollo 10 spacecraft consisted of a Command Service Module, called Charlie Brown, and a Lunar Module, called Snoopy. Today, Charlie Brown is on display at the Science Museum in London, England.

LIFT-OFF
The Apollo 10 spacecraft was launched from Cape Canaveral, known at the time, as Cape Kennedy, at the time. It was the fourth manned Apollo launch in seven months.

on the move

FASTEST
roller coaster
FORMULA
ROSSA

FASTEST ROLLER COASTERS

 Formula Rossa, Abu Dhabi, UAE: 149.1 mph

 Kingda Ka, New Jersey, USA: 128 mph

Top Thrill Dragster, Ohio, USA: 120 mph

 Dodonpa, Yamanashi, Japan: 112 mph

 Red Force, Ferrari Land, Tarragona, Spain: 112 mph

FORMULA ROSSA
World Records
Speed: 149.1 mph
G-force: 1.7 Gs
Acceleration: 4.8 Gs

Thrill seekers hurtle along the Formula Rossa track at 149.1 miles per hour. The high-speed roller coaster is part of Ferrari World in Abu Dhabi, United Arab Emirates. Ferrari World also features the world's largest indoor theme park, at 1.5 million square feet. The Formula Rossa roller coaster seats are red Ferrari-shaped cars that travel from 0 to 62 miles per hour in just two seconds—as fast as a race car. The ride's G-force is so extreme that passengers must wear goggles to protect their eyes. G-force acts on a body due to acceleration and gravity. People can withstand 6 to 8 Gs for short periods. The Formula Rossa G-force is 4.8 Gs during acceleration and 1.7 Gs at maximum speed.

TALLEST
water
coaster

MASSIV

Schlitterbahn Galveston Island Waterpark in Texas is home to the world's tallest water coaster. The aptly named MASSIV measures in at 81 feet and 6.72 inches tall. A water coaster is a water slide that features ascents as well as descents, with riders traveling in rafts or tubes. MASSIV, which the park calls a "monster blaster," was built for the tenth anniversary of the opening of Schlitterbahn Galveston. Riders sit in two-person tubes, which take them over a series of dips and four uphill climbs before dropping into the final landing pool. In April 2016, the park released a virtual version of the ride, allowing people all over the world to see MASSIV from the point of view of a rider.

CIRCUS

OLDEST merry-go-round
FLYING HORSES CAROUSEL

Taking a spin around the Flying Horses Carousel in Martha's Vineyard is a trip back in time. Charles Dare constructed the carousel in 1876 for an amusement park in Coney Island, New York. The carousel moved to Oak Bluffs, Massachusetts, in 1884. A preservation society took over Flying Horses in 1986 to restore the carousel and keep it intact and working. Today, the horses look just as colorful as they did in the 1800s. Their manes are real horsehair, and they have glass eyes. As the horses turn around and around, a 1923 Wurlitzer Band Organ plays old-time music. The Flying Horses Carousel is a National Landmark.

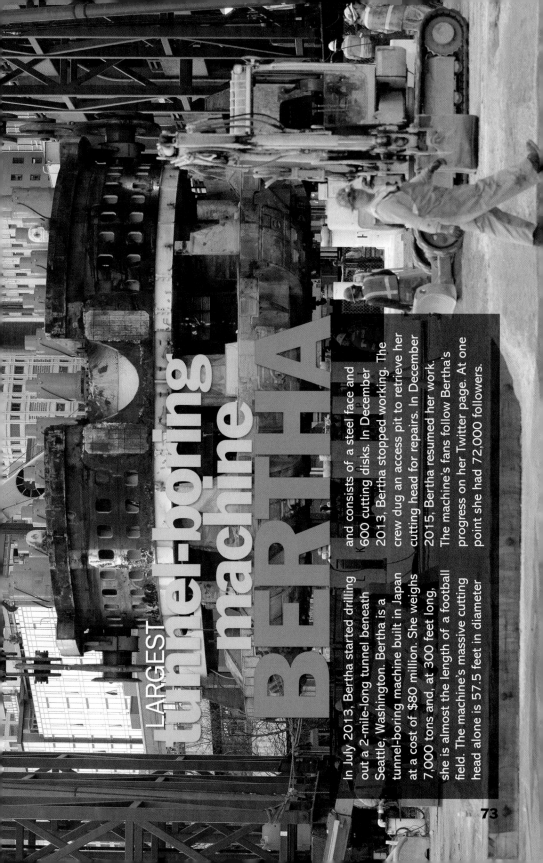

LARGEST
tunnel-boring
machine
BERTHA

In July 2013, Bertha started drilling out a 2-mile-long tunnel beneath Seattle, Washington. Bertha is a tunnel-boring machine built in Japan at a cost of $80 million. She weighs 7,000 tons and, at 300 feet long, she is almost the length of a football field. The machine's massive cutting head alone is 57.5 feet in diameter

and consists of a steel face and 600 cutting disks. In December 2013, Bertha stopped working. The crew dug an access pit to retrieve her cutting head for repairs. In December 2015, Bertha resumed her work. The machine's fans follow Bertha's progress on her Twitter page. At one point she had 72,000 followers.

73

4

super STRUCTURES

SUPER STRUCTURES
TRENDING

MICRO BUILDING
World's smallest house

Scientists in France have built a house that is too small for the naked eye to see. The microscopic building is just twenty micrometers long, about 500,000 times smaller than a human-sized house. Even so, the tiny house has seven windows, a tiled roof, and a chimney. Scientists built the house from silica, using a device that combines robotics, an ion beam, and a gas-injection system.

PRESS PRINT!
3-D printer builds houses

Building a house at the touch of a button? Texas company ICON used its Vulcan 3-D printer to do just that. The Vulcan printed the 350-square-foot house in just forty-eight hours, using layers of concrete. This building method does not need construction workers or expensive materials. ICON plans to build more of these homes in places that need good, affordable housing.

BUILDING WITH BAMBOO
First prize for new home design

It took four hours to build Earl Forlales's bamboo house. The Royal Institute of Chartered Surveyors (RICS) awarded Forlales's Cubo house the top prize for its low cost, use of sustainable materials, and speedy construction. Forlales hopes to start building Cubo houses in Manila and begin rehousing some of the millions of people who live in impoverished areas.

#EIFFELTOWER
Insta-worthy tower

The Eiffel Tower in Paris was the most Instagrammed structure in the world in 2018, with over seven million tags. The 1,063-foot tower is one of the most visited attractions. Some people climb the tower's 1,710 steps while others take an elevator up. Over 1.9 million people visited the tower when it opened in 1889. At the time, it was the tallest structure in the world.

WOODEN TOWERS
World's tallest plyscraper

Mjøstårnet, in Norway, became the tallest plyscraper in the world. Plyscrapers are skyscrapers made from timber. These buildings are a hot new trend in green architecture. The cross-laminated timber is as strong as concrete, but while concrete production emits carbon dioxide, timber stores it. Carbon dioxide is a greenhouse gas that contributes to climate change. Mjøstårnet is 280 feet tall and contains a hotel, restaurant, apartments, and offices.

CITY WITH THE MOST
skyscrapers in the world
HONG KONG

Hong Kong, China, has 317 buildings that reach 500 feet or higher, and three more under construction. Six are 980 feet or higher. The tallest three are the International Commerce Centre (ICC) at 1,588 feet; Two International Finance Centre at 1,352 feet; and Central Plaza at 1,227 feet. Hong Kong's stunning skyline towers above Victoria Harbour. Most of its tallest buildings are on Hong Kong Island, although the other side of the harbor, Kowloon, is growing. Every night a light, laser, and sound show called "A Symphony of Lights" illuminates the sky against a backdrop of about forty of Hong Kong's skyscrapers.

CITIES WITH THE MOST SKYSCRAPERS IN THE WORLD
Number of skyscrapers at 500 feet or higher

Hong Kong, China: 317

New York City, New York, USA: 251

Shanghai, China: 157

Dubai, UAE: 156

LARGEST
sports stadium
RUNGRADO MAY FIRST STADIUM

It took over two years to build Rungrado May First Stadium, a gigantic sports venue that seats up to 114,000 people. The 197-foot-tall stadium opened in 1989 on Rungra Island in North Korea's capital, Pyongyang. The stadium hosts international soccer matches on its natural grass pitch and has other facilities such as an indoor swimming pool; training halls; and a 1,312-foot rubberized running track. The annual Arirang Festival for gymnastics and arts also takes place here.

LARGEST SPORTS STADIUMS
By capacity

Rungrado May First Stadium, North Korea: 114,000

Michigan Stadium, Michigan, USA: 107,601

Beaver Stadium, Pennsylvania, USA: 106,572

Ohio Stadium, Ohio, USA: 104,944

Kyle Field, Texas, USA: 102,733

WORLD'S LARGEST
home in an airliner 727
BOEING

Bruce Campbell's home is not that large, but it is the biggest of its kind. Campbell lives in 1,066 square feet within a grounded 727 Boeing airplane. The airplane no longer has an engine, but Campbell kept the cockpit and its original instruments. He also installed a transparent floor to make the structure of the plane visible. The retired engineer purchased the plane for $100,000 and paid for its transportation to his property in Oregon. Now trees surround the plane instead of sky. Visitors are welcome to take a tour.

WORLD'S LARGEST
house shaped like a VW beetle
VOGLREITER RESIDENCE

Architect Markus Voglreiter turned an ordinary home in Gnigl, near Salzburg, Austria, into an attention-grabbing showpiece: a Volkswagen Beetle–shaped house. The eco-friendly home, completed in 2003, is energy efficient and offers separate, comfortable living quarters. The car-shaped extension measures 950 square feet and is over 32 feet tall. At night, two of the home's windows look like car headlights.

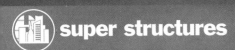

super structures

Just one night at the Hotel President Wilson in Geneva, Switzerland, could set you back $80,000. That is the going rate for the hotel's Royal Penthouse Suite, making it the most expensive hotel in the world. At 18,083 square feet, the suite is also Europe's largest. Occupying the entire eighth floor of the hotel, the Royal Penthouse Suite has terraces overlooking Lake Geneva and rooms for up to twelve guests. Luxury amenities include a billiard table, a private gym, a telescope for stargazing at night, a Steinway grand piano, and a collection of antique books. Since guests include top celebrities and heads of state, the suite naturally comes with maximum-security features, such as a private elevator, a reinforced safe, and bulletproof glass.

WORLD'S MOST
expensive hotel
HOTEL PRESIDENT WILSON

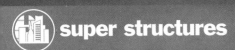

WORLD'S FIRST
hotel made of salt
PALACIO DE SAL

Hotel Palacio de Sal in Uyuni, Bolivia, is the first hotel in the world made completely out of salt. Originally built in 1998, construction began on the new Palacio de Sal in 2004. The hotel overlooks the biggest salt flat in the world, Salar de Uyuni, which covers 4,086 square miles. Builders used around one million blocks of salt to create the hotel walls, floors, ceilings, and furniture. Some of the hotel's thirty rooms have igloo-shaped roofs. The salt flats lie in an area once covered by Lago Minchin, an ancient salt lake. When the lake dried up, it left salt pans, one of which was the Salar de Uyuni.

ANOTHER STRANGE PLACE TO STAY
Hotel shaped like a dog: Dog Bark Park Inn in Cottonwood, Idaho, where you can sleep inside a wooden beagle that measures 33 feet tall and 16 feet wide.

DUBAI'S BURJ KHALIFA WORLD RECORDS:

Tallest building: 2,717 feet

Most floors: 160

Fastest elevators: 55 feet per second

Laid end to end, the steel used here would stretch one-quarter of the way around the world!

BURJ KHALIFA

IT CAN SWAY UP TO 3.9 FEET!

GOING UP!

THE UPPER SECTION IS STEEL FRAMED, SO IT'S POSSIBLE TO MAKE IT TALLER. DURING BUILDING, ITS HEIGHT WAS RAISED THREE TIMES.

WORLD'S LARGEST freestanding building

NEW CENTURY GLOBAL CENTER

The New Century Global Center in Chengdu, southwestern China, is an enormous 18.9 million square feet. That's nearly three times the size of the Pentagon, in Arlington, Virginia. Completed in 2013, the structure is 328 feet tall; 1,640 feet long; and 1,312 feet deep. The multiuse building houses a 4.3-million-square-foot shopping mall, two hotels, an Olympic-size ice rink, a fourteen-screen IMAX cinema complex, and offices. It even has its own Paradise Island, a beach resort complete with artificial sun.

WORLD'S LARGEST
swimming pool
CITYSTARS POOL

The Citystars lagoon in Sharm el-Sheikh, Egypt, stretches over 30 acres. It was created by Crystal Lagoons, the same company that built the former record holder at San Alfonso del Mar in Chile. The lagoon at Sharm el-Sheikh cost $5.5 million to create and is designed to be sustainable, using salt water from local underground aquifers. The creators purify this water not just for recreation but also to provide clean, fresh water to the surrounding community.

LARGEST SWIMMING POOLS
Size in acres

Citystars, Sharm el-Sheikh, Egypt: 30

San Alfonso del Mar, Algarrobo, Chile: 19.7

Seagaia Ocean Dome, Miyazaki, Japan (closed): 7.4

Dead Sea, Yuncheng, China: 7.4

Orthlieb Pool, Casablanca, Morocco: 3.7

WORLD'S TALLEST
tree house
THE MINISTER'S HOUSE

Minister Horace Burgess began building his tree house in 1993 and took many years erecting the towering, ten-story, 97-foot-high structure. The main support is an 80-foot-tall white oak tree, while six other trees provide reinforcement. The Minister's House, as it is known, is in a wooded area in Crossville, Tennessee, and includes a church topped by a chime tower. Thousands came to visit the amazing attraction every year, until the state fire marshal closed the tree house permanently in 2012 due to fire hazards.

WORLD'S
greenest city
SINGAPORE

According to a new study from Treepedia, Singapore has the highest percentage of urban greenery in the world. Treepedia is the work of the Senseable City Laboratory at Massachusetts Institute of Technology (MIT). By analyzing panoramas posted on Google Street View, the Treepedia program assesses the level of vegetation in a city and rates it on a scale of 0–100 in its Green View Index (GVI). The program shows the real level of greenery in the streets on which city people live and work. The people behind Treepedia hope to raise greater awareness in cities where trees are lacking and to encourage developers to include them in future projects.

GREENEST CITIES
Treepedia's GVI rating

🌳🌳🌳🌳🌳 Singapore: 29.3%

🌳🌳🌳🌳 Sydney, Australia: 25.9%

🌳🌳🌳 Vancouver, Canada: 25.9%

🌳🌳 Cambridge, MA, USA: 25.3%

🌳 Durban, South Africa: 23.7%

WORLD'S LARGEST

vertical garden

KAOHSIUNG CITY

A vertical garden in Kaohsiung City, Taiwan, is the largest in the world at 27,922 square feet, almost the size of ten tennis courts! The garden, also called a "green wall," was completed in June 2015 and forms part of a fence around Cleanaway Company Ltd., a waste-disposal company. Construction took about two months and more than 100,000 plants. From afar, the panorama shows a landscape at sunset, with a bright red sun. However, green walls are not only beautiful; they help to lower pollution and carbon-dioxide emissions.

WORLD'S LARGEST
greenhouse
EDEN PROJECT

The Eden Project sprawls over 32 acres of land in the countryside of Cornwall, England. Nestled in the cavity of a china clay pit, it's the world's largest greenhouse and has been open since 2003. Eight interlinked, transparent domes house two distinct biomes. The first is a rainforest region and the second is Mediterranean. Each has around one thousand plant varieties. Visitors can see a further three thousand different plants in the 20 acres of outdoor gardens. During construction, the Eden Project used a record-breaking 230 miles of scaffolding.

COUNTRY WITH THE MOST GREENHOUSES
The Netherlands: Greenhouses cover more than 25 square miles of the country's entire area.

WORLD'S LARGEST tomb of a known individual
QIN SHI HUANG'S TOMB

FIRST EMPEROR OF CHINA

Emperor Qin Shi Huang was the first emperor of a unified China. Before his rule, the territory had been a collection of independent states. He was just forty-nine years old when he died.

QIN SHI HUANG'S TOMB STATS

1974
YEAR OF DISCOVERY

36
NUMBER OF YEARS IT TOOK TO CREATE

8,000
TOTAL NUMBER OF FIGURES FOUND

221–207
DURATION OF THE QIN DYNASTY, BCE

Emperor Qin Shi Huang ruled China from 221 to 207 BCE. In 1974, people digging a well in the fields northeast of Xi'an, in Shaanxi province, accidentally discovered the ancient tomb. Further investigation by archaeologists revealed a burial complex over 20 square miles. A large pit contained 6,000 life-size terra-cotta warrior figures, each one different from the next and dressed according to rank. A second and third pit contained 2,000 more figures; clay horses; about 40,000 bronze weapons; and other artifacts. Historians think that 700,000 people worked for about thirty-six years to create this incredible mausoleum. The emperor's tomb remains sealed to preserve its contents and to protect workers from possible hazards, such as chemical poisoning from mercury in the surrounding soil.

Founded in the late ninth century, Prague Castle is officially the largest coherent castle complex in the world. Covering 750,000 square feet, the castle grounds span enough land for seven football fields, with buildings in various architectural styles that have been added and renovated during past centuries. Formerly the home of kings and emperors, the castle is now occupied by the president of the Czech Republic and his family and is also open to tourists. The palace contains four churches, including the famous St. Vitus Cathedral.

WORLD'S LARGEST castle
PRAGUE CASTLE

WORLD'S LARGEST sandcastle
DUISBURG, GERMANY

schauinsland reisen

On September 1, 2017, German tour operator and travel agency Schauinsland-Reisen GmbH built a sandcastle measuring 54 feet 9 inches—the tallest ever recorded—in the city of Duisburg. The team that created the sandcastle spent almost a month doing so, using around 3,850 metric tons of sand that had been delivered by 168 trucks.

The design of the sandcastle included some of the most famous tourist spots across the globe, including the Leaning Tower of Pisa and the Acropolis in Athens. Measured using laser technology, the sandcastle was half a foot taller than that of the previous record set on the beach at Puri, Odisha, India, just seven months earlier.

OMER TOWER

TEL AVIV, ISRAEL

WORLD'S TALLEST
LEGO® tower

During the last few weeks of December 2017, a LEGO® tower measuring 117 feet and 11 inches tall was built in Rabin Square, Tel Aviv, Israel. Several thousand volunteers came together to build the sky-high monument in memory of Omer Sayag, an eight-year-old boy who died of cancer in 2014. Tel Aviv City Hall worked with Young Engineers, an organization that promotes learning through building with toy bricks. They used over half a million LEGO® bricks in total. Once complete, it broke the record for the tallest-ever LEGO® tower, beating the previous record of 116 feet, 4 inches, set in Günzberg, Germany, in June 2016, by 19 inches.

WORLD'S LARGEST sculpture cut from a single piece of stone

SPHINX

The Great Sphinx stands guard near three large pyramids in Giza, Egypt. Historians believe ancient people created the sculpture about 4,500 years ago for the pharaoh Khafre. They carved the sphinx from one mass of limestone in the desert floor, creating a sculpture about 66 feet high and 240 feet long. It has the head of a pharaoh and the body of a lion. The sculpture may represent Ruti, a twin lion god from ancient myths that protected the sun god, Ra, and guarded entrances to the underworld. Sand has covered and preserved the Great Sphinx, but over many years, wind and humidity have worn parts of the soft limestone away, some of which have been restored using blocks of sand and quicklime.

GREAT SPHINX FACTS
Age: 4,500 years (estimated)
Length: 240 feet
Height: 66 feet

5

HIGH TECH
TRENDING#↑

ROYAL RECORD
Prince Harry and Duchess Meghan join Instagram

After creating their joint Instagram account in April 2019, the Duke and Duchess of Sussex had one million followers in just five hours and forty-five minutes. This beat the previous record of K-pop star Kang Daniel. Their first post was a series of photos that earned almost 900,000 likes within the first two days.

PAINTING SELF DESTRUCTS
Banksy art shredded

Girl with Balloon, a painting by British artist Banksy, destroyed itself after selling for $1.4 million dollars. The auctioneer at Sotheby's, in London, announced the painting was sold, and seconds later *Girl with Balloon* started shredding inside its frame and stopped about halfway through. Later, Banksy revealed that he had built a shredder inside the frame in case the painting ever sold at auction.

SWEET PHOTO OPS
Art museums made for the 'gram

A new kind of art museum became the go-to place for the best Instagram photos in 2018. Candytopia, a pop-up museum in New York and San Francisco, provided the perfect background for Instagram poses. Its exhibits included candy "art," such as a gummy bear sculpture and a marshmallow pool for people to jump into. Candytopia followed the success of the Museum of Ice Cream and the Color Factory.

BATTLING FOR BILLIONS
Fortnite earns more than any other game

The online game *Fortnite* earned $2.4 billion in 2018, more than any game in history has earned in one year. The game is free to download and play, but players buy extras such as digital outfits for the game's avatars. *Fortnite* works across different platforms, which helped build the popularity to more than 200 million people around the world.

DISLIKE!
YouTube "Rewind" gets thumbs down

Almost 10.1 million people hit "dislike" under YouTube's annual "Rewind" video for 2018, making the video the most disliked on YouTube ever. Justin Bieber fans were happy with this new record. It pushed Bieber's 2010 "Baby" video from the most disliked spot, where it has been for many years with 9.9 million dislikes. YouTube's "Rewind" is a recap of the year's highlights on the social media site.

CELEBRITY WITH THE MOST
Instagram followers
CRISTIANO RONALDO

Portuguese soccer icon Cristiano Ronaldo overtook Selena Gomez to become the most followed celebrity on Instagram in 2018. The star gained more than forty million followers in 2018 and had two of the site's top ten-most-liked posts of the year. That same year, Ronaldo won a third consecutive UEFA Champions League (the annual tournament for the best teams across Europe) with Real Madrid before transferring to Italian side Juventus for 112 million euros ($131 million).

CELEBRITIES WITH THE MOST INSTAGRAM FOLLOWERS 2018
In millions of followers

- Cristiano Ronaldo: 157
- Ariana Grande: 148
- Selena Gomez: 147
- The Rock: 134
- Kim Kardashian West: 104

MOST RETWEETED
photo ever
ELLEN DEGENERES

Ellen DeGeneres's selfie taken at the 2014 Oscars is the most Retweeted photo ever. The photo, which pictures DeGeneres, Bradley Cooper, Jennifer Lawrence, and many other celebrities, has over 3.3 million Retweets. In just over one hour, the post was Retweeted more than 1 million times. The rush of activity on Twitter crashed the social networking site for a short time. Before the Oscar selfie took over Twitter, President Obama held the record for the most Retweeted photo. On November 6, 2012, the president posted an election victory photo and Tweet that has been Retweeted over 900,000 times.

TOP-GROSSING
iphone gaming app
CLASH OF CLANS

TOP-GROSSING IPHONE GAMING APPS
Daily revenue in U.S. dollars (as of May 2019)

Clash of Clans: 1,547,320

Fortnite: 1,500,901

Candy Crush Saga: 1,186,640

Clash Royale: 574,954

ROBLOX: 366,856

The free online gaming app *Clash of Clans* had the highest daily revenue of all iPhone gaming apps in 2018–19. Estimates suggest the game generates around $1.55 million a day. Initially released in 2012, the app involves gamers developing clan bases, which they must defend against invading forces. It's as simple as that! However, the action continues when players leave the game, which means they have to check in to make sure their clan is not under attack. Gaming critics and fans believe this is a major factor in the game's success.

MOST-VIEWED
YouTube
video ever
"DESPACITO"

In 2017, "Despacito"
by Luis Fonsi and Daddy
Yankee (later remixed by
Justin Bieber) became the world's
most viewed YouTube video ever. With
more than six billion views and counting, the video broke
the record on approaching the three billion mark in August
2017. The record knocked Wiz Khalifa and Charlie Puth's
"See You Again" from the top spot. "See You Again" had
only just taken the crown from Psy's "Gangnam Style."

MOST-USED
Instagram
hashtag

The most popular hashtag on Instagram in 2018 was used to caption a variety of photographs—romantic selfies, cute animals, even shots of new shoes. The picture-sharing platform displays more than 1.6 billion posts that use the tag #love, and the number continues to grow. Taking second spot on the listings in 2018, was #instagood, for photos that are just "too good" not to share. Also rising in the ranks are #me and #cute, which speak for themselves.

MOST POPULAR
beauty and style vlogger
YUYA

The Mexican vlogger Mariand Castrejón, aka Yuya, ranks as YouTube's most popular beauty vlogger based on channel subscriptions. When the ratings were taken in May 2019, Yuya had more than twenty-three million subscribers, compared to the next highest in popularity, Jeffree Star, with just over fourteen million. According to Social Blade—YouTube's stats website—Yuya can make anywhere between $4,900 to $77,700 a month from her videos. The young woman started her channel in 2009 after winning a makeup video contest. Since that time she has posted numerous videos on women's beauty and has released her own line of makeup.

TOP BEAUTY AND STYLE VLOGGERS 2018
Subscribers in millions (as of May 2019)

Yuya: 23.59

Jeffree Star: 14.24

Zoella: 11.82

Nikkie Tutorials: 11.79

Bethany Mota: 10.34

PRODUCT WITH THE MOST
Facebook fans
SAMSUNG

South Korean tech giant Samsung has more Facebook likes than any other branded product. The company's Facebook page is mostly used to share videos showcasing new products and highlighting the features of its phones. As of March 2019, it already had as many as ten times more Facebook likes than its biggest rival in the smartphone industry, Apple Inc.

PRODUCTS WITH THE MOST FACEBOOK FANS
In millions of fans, as of May 2019

  Samsung: 156.2

 Coca-Cola: 107.4

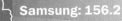 Red Bull: 49

 Nike Football: 44.9

    Converse All Star: 44.9

CRISTIANO RONALDO

PERSON WITH THE MOST
Facebook "likes"

Soccer pro Cristiano Ronaldo retained the top spot on Facebook in 2018 with over 122 million fans. Born in 1985, Ronaldo plays for both the Portuguese national team and Spanish powerhouse Real Madrid. As a teenager, Ronaldo's soccer skills were so impressive that British team Manchester United signed him for around $17 million. In 2008, Ronaldo earned the honor of FIFA World Player of the Year, and in 2017 he won the Ballon d'Or (Golden Ball) award for the fifth time.

PEOPLE WITH THE MOST FACEBOOK FANS
In millions of fans, as of May 2019

Cristiano Ronaldo: 122.46

Shakira: 103.51

Vin Diesel: 100.42

Lionel Messi: 89.56

Eminem: 89.36

DOG WITH THE MOST
Instagram followers JIFFPOM

On May 3, 2017, and with 4.8 million followers, Jiffpom broke the Guinness World Record for being the most popular dog on Instagram. Almost two years later, in April 2019, the dog's follower count had risen to nine million. Jiffpom's owner posts snapshots of the fluffy little dog dressed in a wide range of cute outfits and Jiffpom even has a website. The Pomeranian from the United States has other records to boast of, too. At one time, he held the record for the fastest dog to cover a distance of 16.4 feet on his front legs (7.76 seconds). Another time, he was the record holder for covering 32.8 feet on his hind legs (6.56 seconds).

CAT WITH THE MOST Instagram followers NALA CAT

With a total of nine million followers, Nala Cat topped the bill as Instagram's most popular cat in 2018. Adopted from a shelter at just five months old, the Siamese-Tabby mix with bright blue eyes is now eight years old. Visitors to Nala's website can meet other members of her cat family—White Coffee, Stella and Steve, and Luna Rose. Fans can also track events in the cats' lives by reading Nala's blog.

BESTSELLING
video game ever

Tetris, developed by Russian computer scientist Alexey Pajitnov in 1984, has sold over 170 million copies worldwide—more than any other game. It has been available on almost every video game console since its creation and has seen a resurgence in sales as an app for cell phones and tablets. The iconic puzzle game was the first video game to be exported from the Soviet Union to the United States, the first to be played in outer space, and is often listed as one of the best video games of all time. In 2019, Nintendo released *Tetris 99* for Nintendo Switch—a multiplayer version of the game that sees ninety-nine players compete online.

TETRIS

According to Newzoo, *League of Legends* was the most popular online game in 2018. Ranking games by the number of unique players each month, *League of Legends* came out on top time and again. Riot Games created *League of Legends* in 2009, and it quickly became one of the most popular MOBA—Multiplayer Online Battle Arena—games. The game is free to play, although players purchase points to buy "champions," "boosts," and other virtual items to help them on the battlefield. The game is popular among eSports players, with teams competing in the *League of Legends* World Championship contests for big money.

MOST POPULAR
online game

LEAGUE OF LEGENDS

MOST POPULAR ONLINE GAMES
World ranking as of May 2019
1. *League of Legends*
2. *Hearthstone*
3. *Minecraft*
4. *Counter-Strike: Global Offensive*
5. *Fortnite*

BESTSELLING
games console
of 2018
NINTENDO
SWITCH

The Nintendo Switch marginally beat out Sony's PlayStation 4 to become the bestselling video game console of 2018 in the United States. While slightly more PS4 consoles sold worldwide (17.7 million as opposed to 17.4 million), Nintendo's home console reigned supreme in the U.S. market, with six of the twenty bestselling games of the year being exclusive to the Switch. The PS4 led the Switch in units sold until November, when the release of Switch exclusive *Pokémon* games and *Super Smash Bros. Ultimate* boosted sales.

BESTSELLING
video game franchise of all time
MARIO

Nintendo's Mario franchise has sold 628 million units since the first game was released in 1981. Since then, Mario, his brother Luigi, and other characters like Princess Peach and Yoshi have become household names, starring in a number of games across consoles. In the early games, like *Super Mario World*, players jump over obstacles, collect tokens, and capture flags as Mario journeys through the Mushroom Kingdom to save the princess. The franchise has since diversified to include other popular games, such as *Mario Kart*, a racing game showcasing the inhabitants and landscapes of Mushroom Kingdom.

BESTSELLING VIDEO GAME FRANCHISES
Units sold in millions, as of May 2019

 **Mario (Nintendo): 628**

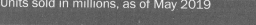 **Pokémon (Game Freak): 302**

 **Grand Theft Auto (Rockstar North): 270**

 FIFA Soccer: 260

 **Call of Duty (Infinity Ward): 250**

MINE

BIGGEST CONVENTION **for a single video game**

MINEFAIRE 2016

12,140

NUMBER OF PEOPLE ATTENDING
MINEFAIRE: 12,140

150,000

TOTAL AREA, IN SQUARE FEET,
OF *MINECRAFT*-CENTERED
ATTRACTIONS: 150,000

3

NUMBER OF GUINNESS WORLD
RECORDS BROKEN AT THE FAIR: 3

According to Guinness World Records, Minefaire 2016, a gathering of *Minecraft* fans, was the biggest convention ever for a single video game. Held October 15–16, at the Greater Philadelphia Expo Center in Oaks, Pennsylvania, the event attracted 12,140 people. Game developer Markus Persson created *Minecraft* in 2009 and sold it to Microsoft in 2014 for $2.5 billion. Gamers can play alone or with other players online. The game involves breaking and placing blocks to build whatever gamers can imagine—from simple constructions to huge virtual worlds. Attendance was not the only element of Minefaire to gain world-record status. On October 15 the largest-ever *Minecraft* architecture lesson attracted 342 attendees, and American gamer Lestat Wade broke the record for building the tallest staircase in *Minecraft* in one minute.

OPPORTUNITY

rover on mars

LONGEST-SURVIVING

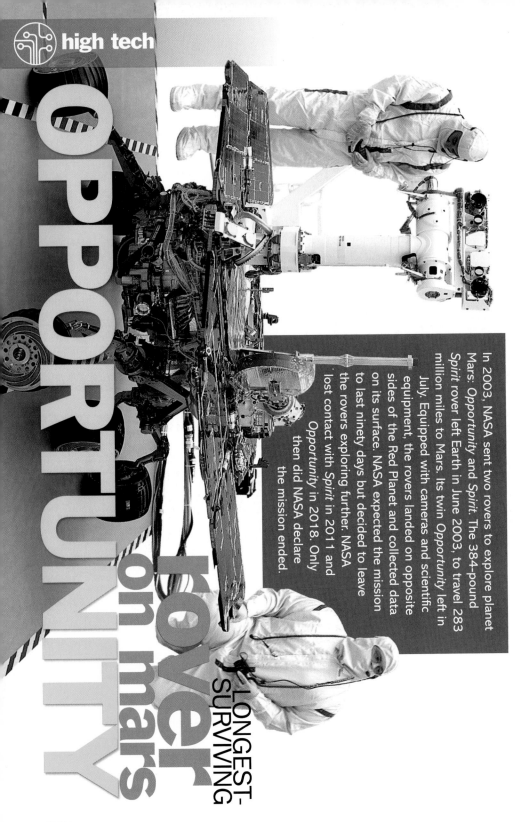

In 2003, NASA sent two rovers to explore planet Mars: *Opportunity* and *Spirit*. The 384-pound *Spirit* rover left Earth in June 2003, to travel 283 million miles to Mars. Its twin *Opportunity* left in July. Equipped with cameras and scientific equipment, the rovers landed on opposite sides of the Red Planet and collected data on its surface. NASA expected the mission to last ninety days but decided to leave the rovers exploring further. NASA lost contact with *Spirit* in 2011 and *Opportunity* in 2018. Only then did NASA declare the mission ended.

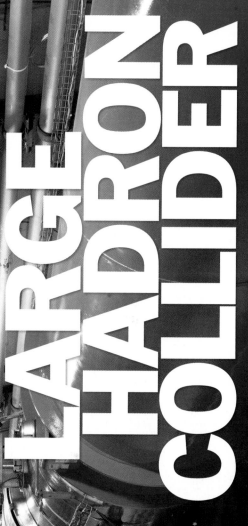

LARGE HADRON COLLIDER

The Large Hadron Collider (LHC) is a 16-mile, ring-shaped machine that sits 328 feet below ground on the French/Swiss border. In 2008, the European Organization for Nuclear Research (CERN) switched on the machine that thousands of scientists and engineers spent years building. They hope that the gigantic collider will explain many mysteries of the universe by examining its tiniest particles, called hadrons. The machine makes these particles travel almost at the speed of light and records what happens when they collide. The aim is to examine various scientific theories, including the idea that the universe originated in a massive cosmic explosion known as the Big Bang.

LARGEST single machine

119

Fanny is a massive 26-foot-high, 51-foot-long, fire-breathing dragon. She is also the world's biggest walking robot. In 2012, a German company designed and built Fanny using both hydraulic and electronic parts. She is radio remote-controlled with nine controllers, while 238 sensors allow the robot to assess her environment. She does this while walking on her four legs or stretching wings that span 39 feet. Powered by a 140-horsepower diesel engine, Fanny weighs a hefty 24,250 pounds—as much as two elephants—and breathes real fire using 24 pounds of liquid gas.

BIGGEST
walking robot
FANNY

FANNY STATS:

09/27/2012

DATE OF FANNY'S LAUNCH

26′ 10″

FANNY'S HEIGHT: in feet and inches

51′ 6″

FANNY'S LENGTH: in feet and inches

12′

FANNY'S BODY WIDTH: in feet

39′

FANNY'S WINGSPAN: in feet

WORLD'S SMALLEST surgical robot VERSIUS

British robot specialists Cambridge Medical Robotics developed the world's smallest surgical robot in 2017. Operated by a surgeon using a console guide with a 3-D screen, the robot is able to carry out keyhole surgery. The scientists modeled the robot, called Versius, on the human arm, giving it similar wrist joints to allow maximum flexibility. Keyhole surgery involves making very small cuts on the surface of a person's body, through which a surgeon can operate. The recovery time of the patient is usually quicker when operated on in this way.

FASTEST
remote-controlled car

BLACK KNIGHT

Built and driven by Anthony Lovering from the United Kingdom, and reaching speeds of more than 200 miles per hour, Black Knight is the world's fastest rocket-powered remote-controlled car. On May 4, 2016, Black Knight hit a speed of 210.11 mph at Snowdonia Aerospace LLP, in Llanbedr, U.K., setting a Guinness World Record that remains unbeaten. Lovering is cofounder of an organization called ROSSA, the Radio Operated Scale Speed Association, which holds events all over the world to find the fastest remote-controlled vehicles.

amazing ANIMALS

 **amazing animals**

WILD ANIMALS
TRENDING#

#HOTDUCK
Colorful duck becomes New York celebrity

A Mandarin duck arrived in a Central Park pond and instantly became a hit online. The duck was not native to the park and may have escaped from a zoo or private owner. Crowds of people tried to get a glimpse of the newcomer. Its bright pink beak, purple chest, and unusual markings made the duck stand out from the plainer ducks on the pond. A bird watcher's Twitter account set up an alert for sightings, and the duck even won its own hashtag, #hotduck.

SPIDERCOON
Raccoon scales skyscraper

A fearless raccoon had the world watching as he scaled a twenty-five-story building in St. Paul, Minnesota. Taking rests on window ledges, the raccoon finally reached the top of the building after almost twenty hours. Crowds gathered on the street below and thousands followed the raccoon's progress on Twitter and Facebook. When the raccoon reached the roof at around 3 a.m., rescuers were there to give him food and take him to safety.

ALL THAT JAZZ
Sharks prefer jazz tunes

Sharks have amazing hearing, and it turns out they prefer to listen to jazz music over classical! Researchers at Australia's Macquarie University put some food at one end of the shark tank and played jazz music at that end. Sharks learned to swim toward the sound of jazz to get a tasty treat. When the researchers played classical music at the same location, the sharks were not interested. In fact, they swam in the opposite direction.

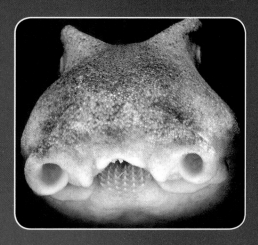

EGGTASTIC
Hen's egg photo gets all the likes

A record fifty-three million Instagram users double-tapped on a simple photo of a brown egg. This massive number of likes beat the previous record of 18.5 million for a photo of Kylie Jenner's baby daughter, Stormi. The egg photo, taken by Serghei Platanov, first appeared on a stock photo website in 2015. In January 2019, Chris Godfrey created the official @world_egg_account, and posted the egg photo to see if the post could break Jenner's record.

WILD COMICS
Squirrel wins comedy photo award

The funniest wildlife photo of the year was the "Caught in the Act" squirrel. The image beat out thousands of submissions and forty other finalists to win the Comedy Wildlife Photography's yearly contest. Mary McGowan from Florida won the top prize for her surprised squirrel. Other hilarious animal photos included two lizards dancing, a smiling blue shark, and a rhino that looks like it's wearing a tutu.

WORLD'S
sleepiest
animal
KOALA

Australia's koala sleeps for up to twenty hours a day and still manages to look sleepy when awake. This is due to the koala's unbelievably monotonous diet. It feeds, mostly at night, on the aromatic leaves of eucalyptus trees. The leaves have little nutritional or calorific value, so the marsupial saves energy by snoozing. It jams its rear end into a fork in the branches of its favorite tree so it cannot fall out while snoozing.

WORLD'S
best glider

Flying squirrels are champion animal gliders. The Japanese giant flying squirrel has been scientifically recorded making flights of up to 164 feet from tree to tree. These creatures have been estimated to make 656-foot flights when flying downhill. The squirrel remains aloft using a special flap of skin on either side of its body, which stretches between wrist and ankle. Its fluffy tail acts as a stabilizer to keep it steady, and the squirrel changes direction by twisting its wrists and moving its limbs.

FLYING SQUIRREL

WORLD'S GLIDERS
Distance in feet

Flying squirrel: 656

Flying fish: 655

Colugo, or flying lemur: 230

Draco, or flying lizard: 197

Flying squid: 164

WORLD'S heaviest land mammal

AFRICAN BUSH ELEPHANT

The African bush elephant is the world's largest living land animal. The biggest known bush elephant stood 13.8 feet at the shoulder and had an estimated weight of 13.5 tons. It is also the animal with the largest outer ears. The outsize flappers help keep the animal cool on the open savanna. The Asian elephant has much smaller earflaps, because it lives in the forest and is not exposed to the same high temperatures.

WORLD'S
tiniest bat
KITTI'S HOG-NOSED BAT

This little critter, the Kitti's hog-nosed bat, is just 1.3 inches long, with a wingspan of 6.7 inches, and weighs 0.07–0.10 ounces. It's tied for first place as world's smallest mammal with Savi's pygmy shrew, which is longer at 2.1 inches but lighter at 0.04–0.06 ounces. The bat lives in west central Thailand and southeast Myanmar, and the shrew is found from the Mediterranean to Southeast Asia.

WORLD'S LARGEST
primate
GORILLA

The largest living primates are the eastern gorillas, and the biggest subspecies is the very rare mountain gorilla. The tallest known was an adult male silverback, named for the color of the fur on his back. He stood at 6.4 feet tall, but he was an exception—silverbacks generally grow no bigger than 5.9 feet tall. Gorillas have long arms: The record holder had an arm span measuring 8.9 feet, while adult male humans have an average arm span of just 5.9 feet.

THE WORLD'S MOST
colorful monkey
MANDRILL

The male mandrill's face is as flamboyant as his rear end. The vivid colors of both are brightest at breeding time. The colors announce to his rivals that he is an alpha male and he has the right to breed with the females. His exceptionally long and fang-like canine teeth reinforce his dominance. The mandrill is the world's largest monkey, as well as the most colorful.

WORLD'S FASTEST
land animal
CHEETAH

The fastest reliably recorded running speed of any animal was that of a zoo-bred cheetah that reached an incredible 65 miles per hour on a flat surface. Another captive cheetah, this time at Cincinnati Zoo, clocked 61 miles per hour from a standing start in 2012.

More recently, wild cheetahs have been timed while actually hunting their prey in the bush in Botswana. Using GPS technology and special tracking collars, the scientists found that these cheetahs had a top speed of 58 miles per hour over rough terrain.

FASTEST LAND ANIMALS
Speed in miles per hour

Cheetah: 65   Ostrich: 60   Pronghorn: 55   Springbok: 55   Lion: 30

WORLD'S FASTEST fish
BLACK MARLIN

Timing the world's fastest fish relies on how fast a hooked fish pulls the line from a fisherman's reel, so part of its escape is by swimming and part by leaping. Using this method, sailfish, marlin, and swordfish come out on top. A sailfish was credited with 68 miles per hour in the 1930s. A BBC film crew claimed 80 miles per hour for a black marlin in 2001. Then, in a Japanese computer simulation in 2008, scientists calculated that a swordfish could reach 81 miles per hour. But this has not yet been proven in real trials, so the black marlin stays on top for now.

WORLD'S BIGGEST
big cat

TIGER

There are only five big cats: tiger, lion, jaguar, leopard, and snow leopard. The biggest and heaviest is the Siberian, or Amur, tiger, which lives in the taiga (boreal forest) of eastern Siberia, where it hunts deer and wild boar. The largest reliably measured tigers have been about 11.8 feet long and weighed 705 pounds, but there have been claims for larger individuals, such as the male shot in the Sikhote-Alin Mountains in 1950. That tiger weighed 847 pounds.

land animal
HOWLER
MONKEY

The howler monkeys of Latin America are deafening. Males have an especially large hyoid bone. This horseshoe-shaped bone in the neck creates a chamber that makes the monkey's deep guttural growls sound louder for longer.

It is said that their calls can be heard up to 3 miles away. Both males and females call, and they holler mainly in the morning. It is thought that these calls are often one troop telling neighboring troops where they are.

Giraffes living on the savannas of eastern and southern Africa are the world's tallest animals. The tallest known bull giraffe measured 19 feet from the ground to the top of his horns. He could have looked over the top of a London double-decker bus or peered into the upstairs window of a two-story house. Despite having considerably longer necks than we do, giraffes have the same number of neck vertebrae. They also have long legs with which they can either speedily escape from predators or kick them to keep them away.

GIRAFFE STATS

6
HEIGHT OF A CALF AT BIRTH (in feet)

25
AVERAGE LIFE SPAN (in years)

100
ADULT'S DAILY FOOD CONSUMPTION
(in pounds of leaves and twigs)

WORLD'S TALLEST

GIRAFFE

living animal

REACHING GREAT HEIGHTS

A giraffe's tongue can grow up to 21 inches in length. This helps the animal reach leaves on the topmost branches of a tree when it is looking for food.

WORLD'S LONGEST tooth
NARWHAL

The narwhal's "sword" is an enormously elongated spiral tooth, or tusk. It can grow to more than 8.2 feet long. It has been suggested that the tusk serves as an adornment to attract the opposite sex—the larger a male narwhal's tusk, the more attractive he is to females. It is also thought to be a sensory organ that detects changes in the seawater, such as saltiness, which could help the narwhal find food. Observers have also noted that the narwhal uses its tusk to stun prey.

THE WORLD'S LARGEST
living animal
BLUE WHALE

Blue whales are truly colossal. The largest one accurately measured was 110 feet long, and the heaviest weighed 209 tons. They feed on tiny krill, which they filter from the sea. On land, the largest known animal was a Titanosaur—a huge dinosaur that lived in what is now Argentina 101 million years ago. A skeleton found in 2014 suggests the creature was 121 feet long and weighed 77 tons. It belongs to a young Titanosaur, so an adult may have been bigger than a blue whale.

WORLD'S BIGGEST fish
WHALE SHARK

Recognizable from its spotted skin and enormous size, the whale shark is the world's largest living fish. It grows to a maximum length of about 66 feet. Like the blue whale, this fish feeds on some of the smallest creatures: krill, marine larvae, small fish, and fish eggs. The whale shark is also a great traveler: One female was tracked swimming 4,800 miles from Mexico—where hundreds of whale sharks gather each summer to feed—to the middle of the South Atlantic Ocean, where it is thought she may have given birth.

THE SHARK MOST DANGEROUS
to people
GREAT WHITE SHARK

SHARK ATTACKS
Number of humans attacked

Great white: 314

Tiger shark: 11

Bull shark: 100

Sand tiger shark: 29

The great white shark is at the top of the list for the highest number of attacks on people. The largest reliably measured fish was 21 feet long, making it the largest predatory fish in the sea. Its jaws are lined with large, triangular, serrated teeth that can slice through flesh, sinew, and even bone. However, there were just sixty-six reported nonprovoked attacks by sharks of any kind in 2018, and only four of those proved fatal. Humans are not this creature's top food of choice. People don't have enough fat on their bodies. Mature white sharks prefer blubber-rich seals, dolphins, and whales. It is likely that many of the attacks on people are probably cases of mistaken identity.

WORLD'S LARGEST
crustacean
JAPANESE SPIDER CRAB

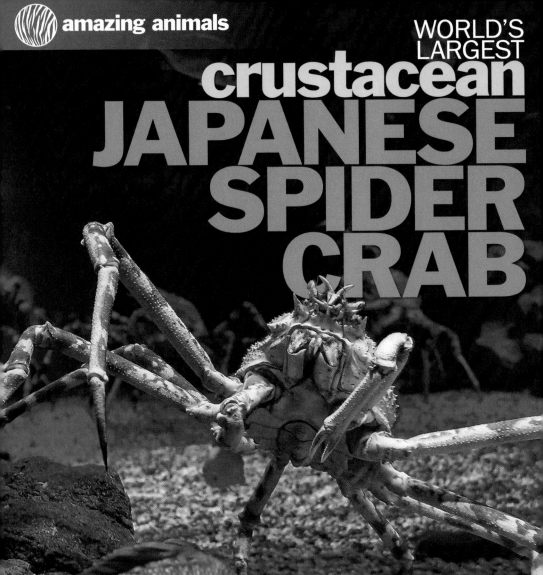

The deepwater Japanese spider crab has the largest leg span of any known crab or lobster. It comes a close second to the American lobster (the world's heaviest crustacean) by weight, and its gangly limbs can be extraordinarily long. The first European to discover this species found two sets of claws, each measuring 10 feet long, propped up against a fisherman's hut. The crab must have been about 22 feet from one claw tip to the other when its limbs were spread apart.

The reticulated python of Indonesia is the world's longest snake. One, called Fragrant Flower, counts among the longest pythons ever discovered. It was living in the wilds of Java until villagers captured it. A local government official confirmed it was 48.8 feet long and weighed 985 pounds. These creatures are constricting snakes: They squeeze the life out of their prey before consuming. In 1999, a 22.9-foot-long python swallowed a sun bear in Balikpapan, East Kalimantan.

WORLD'S
LONGEST
snake
PYTHON

amazing animals

WORLD'S
largest
lizard

KOMODO
DRAGON

There are dragons on Indonesia's Komodo Island, and they're dangerous. The Komodo dragon's jaws are lined with sixty replaceable, serrated, backward-pointing teeth. Its saliva is laced with deadly bacteria and venom that the dragon works into a wound, ensuring its prey will die quickly. Prey can be as big as a pig or deer, because this lizard is the world's largest. It can grow up to 10.3 feet long and weigh 366 pounds.

WORLD'S
deadliest frog

POISON DART FROG

A poison dart frog's skin exudes toxins. There are several species, and the more vivid a frog's color, the more deadly its poison. The skin color warns potential predators that the frogs are not good to eat, although one snake is immune to the chemicals and happily feeds on these creatures. It is thought that the frogs do not manufacture their own poisons, but obtain the chemicals from their diet of ants, millipedes, and mites. The most deadly species to people is also the largest, Colombia's golden poison dart frog. At just one inch long, a single frog has enough poison to kill ten to twenty people.

amazing animals

WORLD'S LARGEST
reptile
SALTWATER CROCODILE

The saltwater crocodile, or "saltie," is the world's largest living reptile. Males can grow to over 20 feet long, but a few old-timers become real monsters. A well-known crocodile in the Segama River, Borneo, left an impression on a sandbank that measured 33 feet. The saltie can be found in areas from eastern India to northeast Australia, where it lives in mangroves, estuaries, and rivers. It is sometimes found out at sea. The saltie is an ambush predator, grabbing any animal that enters its domain—including people. Saltwater crocodiles account for twenty to thirty attacks on people per year, up to half of which are fatal.

"SALTIE" crocodiles can live for up to 70 years in the wild.

NORTH AMERICAN ELF OWL

The North American elf owl is one of three tiny owls vying for this title. It is about 5 inches long and weighs 1.5 ounces. This owl spends winter in Mexico and flies to nest in Arizona and New Mexico in spring. It often occupies cavities excavated by woodpeckers in saguaro cacti. Rivals for the title of smallest owl are Peru's long-whiskered owlet and Mexico's Tamaulipas pygmy owl, which are both a touch shorter but slightly heavier, making the elf owl the smallest of all.

FIVE OF THE WORLD'S OWLS
Height in inches

North American elf owl: 5

Little owl: 8.7

Barn owl: 15

Snowy owl: 28

Great gray owl: 33

WORLD'S
smelliest
bird
HOATZIN

The hoatzin eats leaves, flowers, and fruit, and ferments the food in its crop (a pouch in its esophagus). This habit leaves the bird with a foul odor, which has led people to nickname the hoatzin the "stinkbird." About the size of a pheasant, this bird lives in the Amazon and Orinoco river basins of South America. A hoatzin chick has sharp claws on its wings, like a pterodactyl. If threatened by a snake, the chick jumps from the nest into the water, then uses its wing claws to help it climb back up.

bird with the LONGEST TAIL
RIBBON-TAILED ASTRAPIA

The ribbon-tailed astrapia has the longest feathers in relation to body size of any wild bird. The male, which has a beautiful, iridescent blue-green head, sports a pair of white ribbon-shaped tail feathers that are more than 3.3 feet long—three times the length of its 13-inch-long body. It is one of Papua New Guinea's birds of paradise and lives in the mountain forests of central New Guinea, where males sometimes have to untangle their tails from the foliage before they can fly.

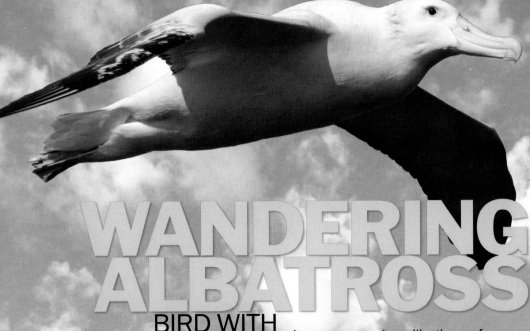

WANDERING ALBATROSS

BIRD WITH THE LONGEST wingspan

Long, narrow wings, like those of a glider aircraft, are the mark of the wandering albatross. The longest authenticated measurement for wingspan was taken in 1965 from an old-timer, its pure white plumage an indication of its age. Its wingspan was 11.9 feet. This seabird rarely flaps its wings but uses the wind and updrafts from waves to soar effortlessly over the ocean.

BIRDS WITH LONG WINGSPANS
Wingspan in feet

Wandering albatross: 11.9

Great white pelican: 11.81

Andean condor: 10.5

Marabou stork: 10.5

Southern royal albatross: 9.8

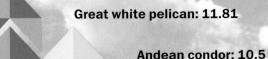

BIRD WITH THE STRONGEST forehead

The helmeted hornbill is a real bruiser. It has a structure, known as a casque, sitting atop its chisel-like bill. Unlike other hornbills, which have hollow casques, the helmeted hornbill has an almost solid one. It is filled with "hornbill ivory," which is even more valuable than elephant ivory in southern Asia. The bill and casque weigh more than 10 percent of the bird's body weight. Males use their heads as battering rams, slamming casques together in fights over territory.

HELMETED HORNBILL

BIRD THAT BUILDS
largest nest
BALD EAGLE

With a wingspan over 6.6 feet, bald eagles need space to land and take off—so their nests can be gargantuan. Over the years, a nest built by a pair of bald eagles in St. Petersburg, Florida, has taken on epic proportions. Measuring 9.5 feet across and 20 feet deep, it is made of sticks, grass, and moss. At one stage it was thought to have weighed at least 2 tons, making it the largest nest ever constructed by a pair of birds. Although one pair nests at a time, these huge structures are often the work of several pairs of birds, each building on top of the work of their predecessors.

THE WORLD'S LARGEST NESTS
Diameter in inches

Bald eagle: 114

Golden eagle: 55

White stork: 57

5.9 in

4.5 in

WORLD'S
largest bird egg
AFRICAN OSTRICH EGG

The ostrich lays the largest eggs of any living bird, yet they are the smallest eggs relative to the size of the mother's body. Each egg is some 5.9 inches long and weighs about 3.5–5 pounds, while the mother is about 6.2 feet tall and the male is about 7.8 feet tall, making the ostrich the world's largest living bird. The female lays about fifty eggs per year, and each egg contains as much yolk and albumen as twenty-four hens' eggs. It takes an hour to soft boil an ostrich egg!

EMPEROR PENGUIN STATS

80
AVERAGE WEIGHT OF AN ADULT:
80 pounds

1,640
DEPTHS AN ADULT CAN SWIM TO:
1,640 feet

22
LENGTH OF TIME UNDERWATER:
Up to 22 minutes

FIVE OF THE WORLD'S PENGUINS
Height in inches

Emperor: 48   King: 39   Gentoo: 35   Macaroni: 28   Galápagos: 19

WORLD'S BIGGEST
penguin

EMPEROR
PENGUIN

At 4 feet tall, the emperor penguin is the world's biggest living penguin. It has a most curious lifestyle, breeding during the long, dark Antarctic winter. The female lays a single egg and carefully passes it to the male. She then heads out to sea to feed, while he remains with the egg balanced on his feet and tucked under a fold of blubber-rich skin. There he stands with all the other penguin dads, huddled together to keep warm in the blizzards and 100-mile-per-hour winds that scour the icy continent. Come spring, the egg hatches, the female returns, and Mom and Dad swap duties, taking turns to feed and care for their fluffy chick.

LARGEST-EVER
bee beard
JUAN CARLOS NOGUEZ ORTIZ

On August 30, 2017, Canadian Juan Carlos Noguez Ortiz made bee-beard history sitting calmly in Yonge-Dundas Square, Toronto, Canada, with thousands of bees on his face. As a crowd of onlookers gathered to watch, he stayed covered for 61 minutes, breaking the previous record of 53 minutes, 34 seconds. Employed by Dickey Bee Honey Farm in Cookstown, Ontario, Canada, Ortiz claimed to have practiced only twice before setting the new record, stating that he "wanted to show people that they don't have to be scared of the bees."

WORLD'S FASTEST

flying
insect

DESERT
LOCUST

Flying insects are difficult to clock, and many impressive speeds have been claimed. The fastest airspeed reliably timed was by fifteen desert locusts that managed an average of 21 miles per hour. Airspeed is the actual speed at which the insect flies. It is different from ground speed, which is often enhanced by favorable winds. A black cutworm moth whizzed along at 70 miles per hour while riding the winds ahead of a cold front. The most shocking measurement, however, is that of a horsefly with an estimated airspeed of 90 miles per hour while chasing an air-gun pellet! The speed, understandably, has not been verified.

WORLD'S DEADLIEST
animal
MOSQUITO

Female mosquitoes live on the blood of birds and mammals—humans included. However, the problem is not what they take, but what they leave behind. In a mosquito's saliva are organisms that cause the world's most deadly illnesses, including malaria, yellow fever, dengue fever, West Nile virus, and encephalitis. It is estimated that mosquitoes transmit diseases to a staggering 700 million people every year, of which 725,000 die. Mosquitoes are the deadliest family of insects on earth.

WORLD'S HEAVIEST spider
GOLIATH BIRD-EATING TARANTULA

FOUR OF THE WORLD'S SPIDERS
Leg span in inches

Giant huntsman spider: 12

Goliath bird-eating tarantula: 11

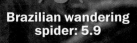

Brazilian wandering spider: 5.9

Golden silk orb-weaver: 5

The size of a dinner plate, the female goliath bird-eating tarantula has a leg span of 11 inches and weighs up to 6.17 ounces. This is the world's heaviest spider and a real nightmare for an arachnophobe (someone with a fear of spiders). Its fangs can pierce a person's skin, but its venom is no worse than a bee sting. The hairs on its body are more of a hazard. When threatened, it rubs its abdomen with its hind legs and releases tiny hairs that cause severe irritation to the skin. Despite its name, this spider does not actually eat birds very often.

PET ANIMALS
TRENDING

ANIMAL INFLUENCERS
Instagram pets gather millions of followers

With Pomeranian Jiffpom leading the way, the top fifteen pet Instagram influencers won a combined twenty-two million followers. The group features @lionelthehog, a tiny hedgehog from South Carolina and @dougthepug, a dog with its own YouTube channel who regularly hangs out with celebrities.

ANIMALS BANNED
No support animals on flights

Delta Airlines banned emotional support animals on flights longer than eight hours in 2018. The move followed a number of incidents involving people trying to bring these pets on board. Unlike service animals, emotional support animals are not registered. Earlier in the year, United Airlines refused to let a woman board a flight with her peacock. The airline claimed the bird's size and weight did not fit within the guidelines. Passengers have also tried to take flights with a squirrel and a pig.

HEAD ABOVE THE CROWD
Giant bovine is Internet sensation

A photo of large, cowlike creature, a Holstein Friesian steer named Knickers, from western Australia, took the Internet by storm. Knickers stands way above the rest of the herd at 6 foot 4 inches tall. The steer weighs about 3,000 pounds, or as much as a small car. Most steers are killed for their meat before they are four years old, but seven-year old Knickers was able to grow to his full height.

NO ROVERS ALLOWED
Weird and funny pet names

The wackiest pet animal names of 2018 were Isabella Miss Worldwide Boo Boo for a dog and Pablo Purrcasso for a cat. Nationwide, a pet health insurance company, compiled the list from over 700,000 of its insured pets. Nationwide based its choices on what it considers the most creative, clever, and quirky names. Coming in at number six on the dog list was Chauncey Von Poops a Lot, while Princess Consuela Bananahammock came in at the same number on the cat list.

STRAPPED IN
Video of dog in a car seat goes viral

A video advertising the Rocketeer car seat won over one billion views on social media in just seven months. The car seat, made by ZuGo Pet, is specially made for dogs to stay safe in case of a car accident. The Rocketeer comes in five sizes to hold dogs up to twenty-five pounds. It also converts to a backpack so owners can carry their smaller dogs.

WORLD'S FLUFFIEST rabbit
ANGORA RABBIT

In most people's opinion, the Angora rabbit is the world's fluffiest bunny. The breed originated in Turkey and is thought to be one of the world's oldest rabbit breeds as well. It became popular with the French court in the mid-eighteenth century. Today it is bred for its long, soft, wool, which is shorn every three to four months. One of the fluffiest bunnies is buff-colored Franchesca, owned by English Angora rabbit expert Dr. Betty Chu. In 2014, Franchesca's fur was measured at 14.37 inches, making a world record that is yet to be beaten.

Thumbelina is a dwarf miniature horse. At just 17.5 inches tall and weighing 60 pounds, she is officially the world's smallest horse. She is stout with unusually short limbs, a far cry from the long-legged Big Jake, the world's tallest horse: a Belgian gelding at 6.9 feet.

WORLD'S
SMALLEST
horse
THUMBELINA

WORLD'S HAIRIEST dog
KOMONDOR

The world's hairiest dog breed is the komondor, or Hungarian sheepdog. It is a powerful dog that was bred originally to guard sheep. Its long, white, dreadlock-like "cords" enable it not only to blend in with the flock but also protect itself from bad weather and bites from wolves. This is a large dog, standing over 27.5 inches at the shoulders. Its hairs are up to 10.6 inches long, giving it the heaviest coat of any dog.

AMERICA'S MOST POPULAR dog breed
LABRADOR

The Labrador retriever holds the top spot as America's most popular breed of dog for a record-breaking 28th consecutive year. Its eager-to-please temperament makes it an ideal companion. The Labrador was originally bred as a gun dog that fetched game birds shot by hunters. Now, aside from being a family pet, it is a favored assistance dog that helps blind people and a good detection dog used by law-enforcement agencies.

AMERICA'S MOST POPULAR DOGS
Rating
1. LABRADOR RETRIEVER
2. GERMAN SHEPHERD
3. GOLDEN RETRIEVER
4. FRENCH BULLDOG
5. BULLDOG
6. BEAGLE
7. POODLE
8. ROTTWEILER
9. GERMAN SHORT-HAIRED POINTER
10. YORKSHIRE TERRIER

WORLD'S TALLEST living dog
FREDDY

At 40.75 inches tall, a Great Dane named Freddy claimed the title world's tallest living dog in December 2016 and holds the record to this day. He lives in the United Kingdom with his owner, Claire Stoneman, and his sister, Fleur. According to Claire, her two pets cost her around $1,400 a year in food alone, with Freddy eating 2.2 pounds of ground beef, 10.5 ounces of liver, and 9 ounces of steak a day. When Freddy stands on his hind legs, he towers over his owner at a height of 90 inches.

WORLD'S

Chihuahuas are the world's smallest dog breed—and the smallest of them all is Miracle Milly, a Chihuahua from Puerto Rico. She measures just 3.8 inches tall, no bigger than a sneaker. The shortest is Heaven Sent Brandy from Largo, Florida, just 6 inches from her nose to the tip of her tail. Chihuahuas originated in Mexico and may have predated the Maya. They are probably descendants of the Techichi, an early companion dog of the Toltec civilization (900–1168 CE).

smallest dog

CHIHUAHUA

AMERICA'S MOST POPULAR
cat breed
RAGDOLL

According to the Cat Fanciers' Association, the Ragdoll melted the hearts of American cat lovers in 2018. Ending the Exotic Shorthair's reign of three consecutive years, the "Raggie" took top spot as the most-registered cat breed of the year. With its lush, silky fur and big blue eyes, this is a cat that loves to be around human beings, relaxing like a "rag doll" when curled up on your lap. The Exotic Shorthair, with its teddy-bear looks, had to settle for second place in the listings.

America's most popular cats
Rating

1. RAGDOLL
2. EXOTIC SHORTHAIR
3. BRITISH SHORTHAIR
4. PERSIAN
5. MAINE COON CAT
6. AMERICAN SHORTHAIR
7. DEVON REX
8. SPHYNX
9. SCOTTISH FOLD
10. ABYSSINIAN

WORLD'S BALDEST cat
SPHYNX

The sphynx breed of cats is famous for its wrinkles and the lack of a normal coat, but it is not entirely hairless. Its skin is like the softest chamois leather, but it has a thin layer of down. It behaves more like a dog than a cat, greeting owners when they come home, and is friendly to strangers. The breed originated in Canada, where a black-and-white cat gave birth to a hairless kitten called Prune in 1966. Subsequent breeding gave rise to the sphynx.

incredible
EARTH

INCREDIBLE EARTH
TRENDING#

EXTREME EARTHQUAKE
Indonesia faced widespread destruction

A magnitude 7.5 earthquake in Indonesia cost at least 2,000 lives in September 2018. Thousands more had serious injuries. The earthquake happened in the country's Sulawesi province. It also destroyed or damaged at least 68,000 homes, rendering many people homeless. The powerful quake triggered a tsunami and landslides around the area and became one of the most extreme disasters of the year.

TEEN ECO-WARRIOR
Swedish teenager leads protest

Swede Greta Thunberg, fifteen years old at the time, inspired a worldwide youth movement for action on climate change. She refused to go to school and camped outside of the Swedish parliament buildings to call her government to action. The school strike went viral and inspired students around the world to stage strikes for action. In early December, Thunberg delivered a stirring speech at the United Nations Climate Conference. In March 2019, more than one million students in 125 countries went on strike.

LOADS OF LAVA
Volcano in Hawaii

Kilauea, an active volcano on the island of Hawaii, bubbled up and erupted on May 3, 2018. Although Kilauea has erupted continuously since 1983, this was its most explosive eruption in 200 years. Volcanic ash clouds burst 30,000 feet into the sky. From May until August, hot lava flowed from the volcano at a rate of 164 feet per day. The volcanic event destroyed more than 700 houses and forced thousands of people to flee from the area.

WAR ON PLASTIC
Attenborough sparks action

Sir David Attenborough's TV series, *Blue Planet II*, inspired a huge increase in the awareness of plastic pollution. After the show aired, 62 percent of people said they would change their plastic habits. The show caused a 169 percent jump in visits to sites such as the Marine Conservation Society. It also prompted government policy changes. In March 2019, *Resource* magazine awarded Attenborough with the number-two spot on their Hot 100 list of influential people.

ICE GIANT
Greenlanders

Dozens of people from Innaarsuit, Greenland, left their village when an enormous iceberg settled nearby. Others waited and watched. The villagers who left lived closest to the sea and were afraid that the iceberg might break up and cause giant waves and flooding. The iceberg was 328 feet high above the water line and 656 feet wide and weighed more than ten million tons, so big that it was visible from space. Eventually, strong winds helped the iceberg drift north away from the village.

OLDEST tree on earth
BRISTLECONE PINE

An unnamed bristlecone pine in the White Mountains of California is the world's oldest continually standing tree. It is 5,066 years old, beating its bristlecone rivals the Methuselah (4,860 years old) and Prometheus (4,848 years old). Sweden is home to an even older tree, a Norway spruce (which are often used as Christmas trees) that took root about 9,550 years ago. However, this tree has not been standing continually, but is long-lived because it can clone itself. When the trunk dies, a new one grows up from the same rootstock, so in theory it could live forever.

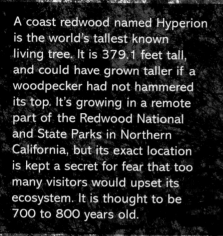

A coast redwood named Hyperion is the world's tallest known living tree. It is 379.1 feet tall, and could have grown taller if a woodpecker had not hammered its top. It's growing in a remote part of the Redwood National and State Parks in Northern California, but its exact location is kept a secret for fear that too many visitors would upset its ecosystem. It is thought to be 700 to 800 years old.

WORLD'S TALLEST TREES

Height in feet

California redwood, California, USA: 379.1

Mountain ash, Styx Valley, Tasmania: 327.4

Coast Douglas-fir, Oregon, USA: 327.3

Sitka spruce, California, USA: 317

Giant sequoia, California, USA: 314

LARGEST AND HEAVIEST
fruit

The world's largest-ever fruit was a cultivated pumpkin grown by Swiss gardener Beni Meier, the first non-American giant pumpkin champion. His winning squash weighed an incredible 2,324 pounds, and Beni had to hire special transportation to take it for weighing in at the October 2014 European Championship Pumpkin Weigh-Off, held in Germany. The seeds of nearly all giant pumpkins can trace their ancestry back to a species of squash that was cultivated by Canadian pumpkin breeder Howard Dill.

PUMPKIN

WORLD'S TOUGHEST leaf
AMAZON WATER LILY

The leaf of the giant Amazon water lily can grow as wide as 8.6 feet across. It has an upturned rim and a waxy, water-repellent upper surface. On the underside of the leaf is a riblike structure that traps air so the leaf floats easily. The ribs are also lined with sharp spines that protect them from aquatic plant eaters. The leaf is so large and so strong that it can support up to ninety-nine pounds in weight.

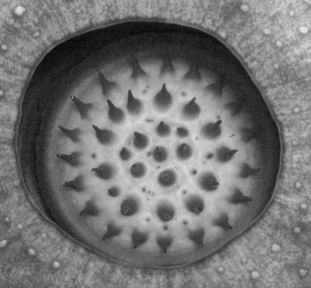

WORLD'S LARGEST
single flower
RAFFLESIA

The scent of dead and decaying meat is not the usual quality sought in a flower, but the flies and beetles on the islands of Borneo and Sumatra love it. *Rafflesia* is known locally as the corpse flower, and at 3.3 feet across, it is the world's largest. It has no obvious stems, leaves, or roots because it is a parasite, and the only time anyone sees it is when it flowers. A female flower has to be fairly close to a male flower for successful pollination, and that is rare, because groups of flowers tend to be either one gender or the other. With forests on the two islands dwindling, the future for *Rafflesia* looks bleak.

WORLD'S MOST DANGEROUS
mushroom
DEATH
CAP

Don't eat the death cap—the warning is in the name. This fungus is responsible for the most deaths by mushroom poisoning and can be found all over the world, including the United States. The mushroom's toxins damage the liver and kidneys, and it is not possible to destroy the dangerous chemicals by cooking, freezing, or drying. The Roman emperor Claudius is thought to have died from death-cap poisoning in 54 CE. He liked to eat salads of Caesar mushrooms, an almost identical edible species, but was served the killer fungus instead.

WORLD'S DEEPEST CAVE
on earth
KRUBERA

The limestone-rich Western Caucasus in the Eurasian country of Georgia have some extraordinary cave systems. Among the caverns there is Krubera, the deepest-known cave on earth. Explorers have descended 7,208 feet from the cave entrance, and they suspect there is even more to explore. The cave is named for the Russian geographer Alexander Kruber, but the Ukrainian cave explorers have dubbed it "Crows' Cave" due to the number of crows that nest around the entrance.

KRUBERA CAVE STATS

1963
YEAR OF DISCOVERY

7,208
DEPTH DISCOVERED TO DATE
(in feet)

2012
YEAR CURRENT DEPTH
ESTABLISHED

EXTRAORDINARY LENGTHS
In order to establish the record-breaking depths of Krubera Cave, diver Gennady Samokhin had to descend as far down as 151 feet in an underwater channel.

THE LARGEST CUT
diamond
GOLDEN
JUBILEE

In 1985, South African miners chanced upon an enormous diamond. Jewel specialists worked for many years to hone it to perfection and fashioned a gem that was a staggering 545.67 carats, the largest cut diamond in the world. Many important leaders have blessed the jewel and the Thai royal family now owns it. For some time, the gem was known as Unnamed Brown, due to its color. Today it goes by the name of Golden Jubilee. If the diamond had been colorless, it would have been worth over $14 million—however, it is a yellow-brown color and worth "only" about $12 million.

WORLD'S GREATEST NUMBER
of geysers
YELLOWSTONE NATIONAL PARK

There are about 1,000 geysers that erupt worldwide, and 540 of them are in Yellowstone National Park, USA. That's the greatest concentration of geysers on earth. The most famous is Old Faithful, which spews out a cloud of steam and hot water to a maximum height of 185 feet every 44 to 125 minutes. Yellowstone's spectacular water display is due to its closeness to molten rock from earth's mantle that rises up to the surface. One day the park could face an eruption 1,000 times as powerful as that of Mt. St. Helens in 1980.

GEYSER FIELDS
Number of geysers

Yellowstone, Idaho/Montana/Wyoming, USA: 540

Valley of Geysers, Kamchatka, Russia: 139

El Tatio, Andes, Chile: 84

Orakei Korako, New Zealand: 33

Hveravellir, Iceland: 16

29,029 feet

Mount Everest's snowy peak is an unbelievable 5.5 miles above sea level. This mega mountain is located in the Himalayas, on the border between Tibet and Nepal. The mountain acquired its official name from surveyor Sir George Everest, but local people know it as Chomolungma (Tibet) or Sagarmatha (Nepal). In 1953, Sir Edmund Hillary and Tenzing Norgay were the first to reach its summit. Now more than 650 people per year manage to make the spectacular climb.

MOUNT EVEREST
is earth's
TALLEST MOUNTAIN
above sea level

WORLD'S TALLEST MOUNTAINS
Height above sea level in feet

Everest: 29,029

K2 (Qogir): 28,251

Kanchenjunga: 28,179

Lhotse: 27,940

Makalu: 27,838

WORLD'S LONGEST
barrier
REEF

Australia's Great Barrier Reef is the only living thing that's clearly visible from space. It stretches along the Queensland coast for 1,400 miles, making it the largest coral reef system in the world. The reef is home to an astounding number of animals: over 600 species of corals alone, 133 species of sharks and rays, and 30 species of whales and dolphins. In recent years, climate change has posed a huge threat to the world's coral reefs, with rising sea temperatures causing areas to die off. The northern half of the Great Barrier Reef suffered particularly in 2016, and scientists fear that more damage is yet to come.

WORLD'S LONGEST BARRIER REEFS
Length in miles

Great Barrier Reef, Australia: 1,400

New Caledonia Barrier Reef, South Pacific: 930

Mesoamerican Barrier Reef, Caribbean: 620

Ningaloo Reef, Western Australia: 162

WORLD'S LARGEST
hot desert
SAHARA DESERT

Sahara means simply "great desert," and great it is: It is the largest hot desert on the planet. It's almost the same size as the United States or China and dominates North Africa from the Atlantic Ocean in the west to the Red Sea in the east. It's extremely dry, with most of the Sahara receiving less than 0.1 inches of rain a year, and some places none at all for several years. It is stiflingly hot, up to 122°F, making it one of the hottest and driest regions in the world.

WORLD'S LARGEST HOT DESERTS
Size in square miles

Sahara Desert, North Africa: 3.63 million

Arabian Desert, Western Asia: 900,000

Great Victoria Desert, Australia: 250,000

Kalahari Desert, Africa: 220,000

Syrian Desert, Western Asia: 190,000

WORLD'S LARGEST lake
CASPIAN SEA

Russia, Kazakhstan, Turkmenistan, Iran, and Azerbaijan border the vast Caspian Sea, the largest inland body of water on earth. Once part of an ancient sea, the lake became landlocked between five and ten million years ago, with occasional fills of salt water as sea levels fluctuated over time. Now it has a surface area of about 149,200 square miles and is home to one of the world's most valuable fish: the beluga sturgeon, the source of beluga caviar, which costs up to $2,250 per pound.

WORLD'S LARGEST LAKES
Area in square miles

Caspian Sea, Europe/Asia: 149,200

Lake Superior, North America: 31,700

Lake Victoria, Africa: 26,600

Lake Huron, North America: 23,000

Lake Michigan, North America: 22,300

WORLD'S LONGEST river
NILE RIVER

People who study rivers cannot agree on the Nile's source—nobody knows where it actually starts. Some say the most likely source is the Kagera River in Burundi, which is the farthest headstream (a stream that is the source of a river) to flow into Lake Victoria. From the lake, the Nile proper heads north across eastern Africa for 4,132 miles to the Mediterranean. Its water is crucial to people living along its banks. They use it to irrigate precious **crops, generate** electricity, and, in the lower

WORLD'S LONGEST RIVERS
Length in miles

Yellow River, China: 3,395

Mississippi–Missouri river system, USA: 3,710

Yangtze River, China: 3,915

Amazon River, South America: 4,000

Nile River, Africa: 4,132

WORLD'S TALLEST surf waves

Many of the world's tallest waves occur at Nazaré, Portugal. In November 2017, this is where Brazilian surfer Rodrigo Koxa rode an 80-foot-high monster wave to seize the world record. The previous record holder, veteran surfer Garrett McNamara from Hawaii, had surfed a 78-foot-tall wave at the same spot in 2011. Nazaré's tallest wave is estimated to have been at least 100 feet tall, but the measurement was not confirmed.

NAZARÉ

WORLD'S TALLEST WAVES
Height in feet (year)

Nazaré, Portugal: 100 (2013)

Caledonia Star, South Atlantic: 98.43 (2001)

Lituya Bay, Alaska: 98 (1958)

Nazaré, Portugal: 78 (2011)

Draupner Oil Platform, Norway: 60.7 (1995)

INCREDIBLE EARTH
TRENDING

HO HO HO, HEAT WAVE!
Australia gets record summer

December 24, 2018, began a record-setting heat wave in Australia. Temperatures in many parts of the country rose to more than 22°F above normal and continued to climb on Christmas Day. January 2019 became the hottest month ever recorded in Australia. In Adelaide, temperatures hit 116°F, the hottest temperature ever recorded in an Australian city.

MIGHTY MICHAEL
Hurricane barrels into Florida

Hurricane Michael became the strongest storm to hit the Florida Panhandle. In October 2018, the hurricane hit Florida with 155 mile-an-hour winds. Michael was the most powerful storm to hit the United States in twenty-five years. The hurricane made landfall in Florida as a Category 4 storm, the second-highest category. Michael wreaked havoc on the coast, killing forty-six people. The storm also left more than one million people across four states without power.

TRAGEDY IN ASIA
Category 5 typhoon

Typhoon Mangkhut brought widespread flooding and damage as it hit Hong Kong, the Philippines, and mainland China. The record-breaking storm left 134 people dead. The typhoon tore through the Philippines, causing landslides and leaving thousands homeless and without power. In China's Guangdong Province, more than 2.4 million people fled their homes before the storm hit. The typhoon also caused major flooding in Thailand.

HOT PLANET
World temperatures rose to record levels

Average temperatures across the globe made 2018 the fourth hottest year on record. Arctic temperatures were the second-warmest in history. The past five years were the hottest period on earth since modern records began. According to NASA and the National Ocean and Atmospheric Association (NOAA), the world was also 1.5°F warmer than a record set between 1951 and 1980.

WILDFIRE IN GREECE
Flames rip through area near Athens

Greece suffered the deadliest wildfire in Europe since 1900. The fire claimed ninety-one lives. Most of those people died in the fire, though some died by drowning. Many people ran into the sea to escape the fire and waited to be rescued. The fire destroyed or damaged more than 2,000 homes. The fire spread quickly due to winds of up to 62 miles per hour and extremely hot, dry conditions.

COLDEST INHABITED PLACE
on earth
OYMYAKON

Extremely low air temperatures of −96.2°F in 1924 and −90°F in 1933 were recorded in the village of Oymyakon in eastern Russia, the lowest temperatures ever recorded in a permanently inhabited area. Only the Antarctic gets colder than this.

The five hundred people living in Oymyakon regularly experience temperatures below zero from September to May, with the December/January/February average falling well below −58°F. The town sits in a valley surrounded by snowy mountains.

COLDEST PLACES ON EARTH

Coldest temperature recorded on earth: Vostok Station, Antarctica at −128.6°F

Coldest inhabited place on earth: Oymyakon, eastern Russia at −96.2°F

Coldest annual mean temperature: Resolute, Canada at 3.7°F

WORLD'S LARGEST ice sculpture
ICE HOTEL

Want to sleep on a bed made of ice in subzero temperatures? That is the prospect for guests at the world's largest ice sculpture—the original Icehotel and art exhibition in Jukkasjärvi, 125 miles north of the Arctic Circle in Sweden. Here, the walls, floors, and ceilings of the sixty-five rooms are made of ice from the local Torne River and snow from the surrounding land. The beds, chairs, and tables—and even the bar and the drinks glasses standing on it—are made of ice. A neighboring ice church hosts one hundred weddings each winter. The hotel is open from December to April, after which it melts back into the wild.

OTHER ICE HOTELS
SnowCastle of Kemi, Finland
Hôtel de Glace, Quebec City, Canada
Bjorli Ice Lodge, Norway
Hotel of Ice at Bâlea Lac, Romania
Ice Village, Shimukappu, Japan

LARGEST
wildfire of 2018
MENDOCINO COMPLEX FIRE

The summer of 2018 saw a series of fires that caused untold destruction across vast areas of California. Notable fires included the Bear Wallow Complex in Siskiyou County, which burned 192,038 acres, and the Basin Complex in Monterey County, which burned 162,818 acres. But no fire rivaled the size of the Mendocino Complex Fire, which started in late July. Recorded as the largest single fire in the state's entire history, the blaze had two flames, the River Fire and the Ranch Fire. Between them they scorched some 459,000 acres, which is about 375,000 football fields big. Records show that eight of the state's largest ten fires have occurred since the start of the twenty-first century.

LARGEST WILDFIRES IN CALIFORNIA HISTORY

(Acres burned)

459,123
Mendocino Complex (July 2018)

281,893
Thomas (December 2017)

273,246
Cedar (October 2003)

271,911
Rush (August 2012)

257,314
Rim (August 2013)

COSTLIEST EVER
With a loss of $16.5 billion, the Camp Fire that raged in Butte County, California, in November 2018 was the year's costliest natural disaster, not only in the United States, but in the world. Almost 14,000 residences were consumed in the flames that burned across 153,000 acres of land.

MOST INTENSE
storm to hit land
HAIYAN

Typhoon Haiyan is one of the most powerful storms ever recorded, and was the strongest-ever tropical storm to hit land. On November 8, 2013, it struck the Philippines, where it was known as Super Typhoon Yolanda.

Wind speeds reached 195 miles per hour, and vast areas of the islands were damaged or destroyed. Around eleven million people were affected: Many were made homeless, and at least 6,300 people were killed.

AMERICA'S MOST costly tornado
THE JOPLIN TORNADO

On May 22, 2011, a multiple-vortex tornado about one mile wide swept through Joplin, Missouri, killing 161 people and injuring more than one thousand others. It was the deadliest tornado in the United States since the 1947 Glazier-Higgins-Woodward tornadoes that swept across Texas, Kansas, and Oklahoma costing 181 people their lives. The Joplin tornado was by far the costliest tornado in U.S. history with $2.8 billion's worth of damage. It was registered as an EF5 category tornado—the most intense kind—with winds in excess of 200 miles per hour. It ripped houses off their foundations and lifted cars and trucks into the air.

HIGHEST TSUNAMI in the United States

LITUYA BAY

On July 9, 1958, a severe 7.8 magnitude earthquake triggered a huge rockslide into the narrow inlet of Lituya Bay, Alaska. The sudden displacement of water caused a mega tsunami, with a crest estimated to be 98 feet tall. The giant wave traveled across the bay and destroyed vegetation up to 1,722 feet above sea level. Five people died, and nearby settlements, docks, and boats were damaged. It was the highest tsunami to be recorded in the United States in modern times.

MOST DESTRUCTIVE
storm surge in the
United States

When Hurricane Katrina slammed into the Louisiana coast in 2005, a storm surge drove the sea almost 12.5 miles inland. New Orleans's hurricane surge protection was breached in fifty-three places, levees failed, boats and barges rammed buildings, and the city and countless neighboring communities were severely flooded. About 80 percent of New Orleans was underwater, close to 1,833 people lost their lives, and an area almost the size of the United Kingdom was devastated. The damage cost an estimated $108 billion. The U.S. Homeland Security secretary described the aftermath of the hurricane as "probably the worst catastrophe, or set of catastrophes" in the country's history.

HURRICANE KATRINA

MOST POWERFUL HURRICANES IN THE UNITED STATES
Wind speed in miles per hour

Labor Day Hurricane (1935): 185

Hurricane Andrew (1992): 177

Hurricane Katrina (2005): 175

Galveston Hurricane (1900): 145

HOTTEST YEAR
on record
2016

Data gathered by NASA's Goddard Institute for Space Studies shows that 2016 was the warmest year since records began in 1880. Global average temperatures were 1.78°F warmer than they were in the mid-twentieth century, and it was the third year in a row that global temperature records were broken, continuing a long-term warming trend. Most scientists agree that this temperature increase is caused by a rise in the greenhouse gas carbon dioxide and other human-made emissions in the atmosphere.

MOST SNOWFALL
in the United States

The greatest depth of snow on record in the United States occurred at Tamarack, near the Bear Valley ski resort in California, on March 11, 1911. The snow reached an incredible 37.8 feet deep. Tamarack also holds the record for the most snowfall in a single month, with 32.5 feet in January 1911. Mount Shasta, California, had the most snowfall in a single storm with 15.75 feet falling from February 13–19, 1959. The most snow in twenty-four hours was a snowfall of 6.3 feet at Silver Lake, Colorado, on April 14–15, 1921.

CALIFORNIA
AND
COLORADO

WORLD'S LARGEST
hailstone
VIVIAN, SOUTH DAKOTA

In August 2010, the town of Vivian, South Dakota, was bombarded by some of the biggest hailstones ever to have fallen out of the sky. They went straight through roofs of houses, smashed car windshields, and stripped vegetation. Among them was a world record breaker, a hailstone the size of a volleyball. It was 8 inches in diameter and weighed 2.2 pounds.

THE HUMAN
lightning conductor

Roy Sullivan was a U.S. park ranger in Shenandoah National Park, Virginia. While going about his duties he was struck by lightning no fewer than seven times. He claimed he was also hit by lightning as a child, making a total of eight lightning strikes. It came to the point that whenever a faraway thunderstorm was heard approaching, his coworkers deliberately distanced themselves from him—just in case!

ROY SULLIVAN

state STATS

STATE STATS
TRENDING#

YEAR OF THE WOMAN
Record year for diversity in government

A dramatic shift happened in the United States government with elections and appointments of women in Congress, the Senate, and the House of Representatives. Altogether, 117 women were elected or appointed to Congress and fifteen to the Senate. Americans also elected 102 women to the House. Among the women were the first two Native Americans and first two Muslims to be elected to Congress.

PRESIDENTIAL MEME
Obama portrait gets social media attention

Barack and Michelle Obama unveiled portraits for the Smithsonian National Portrait Gallery in Washington, D.C. Barack Obama's portrait, by Kehinde Wiley, showed the former president seated against a lush background of leaves and flowers. Thousands took to Twitter to comment and post photoshopped alternatives and memes. One of the most popular combined a GIF of cartoon character Homer Simpson with the presidential portrait.

BREAK-DANCING DAD
Dance moves go viral

Sixty-year-old father of four Ben Hart shot to Internet fame after he displayed his break-dancing skills. Hart started learning to break dance when he was fifty-four as a way to stay in shape. He liked it so much, he kept training. By fifty-nine years old, Hart was dancing in competitions and a video posted on Instagram garnered almost 40,000 views. The Internet success led to a guest appearance and performance on *Good Morning America*.

GUN CONTROL
Student protest gets support from Twitter

More than 1.2 million people across the United States walked to support gun control laws on March 24, 2018. March for Our Lives was the most tweeted about movement of the year. It was also one of the largest American youth movements since the Vietnam War. Student survivors of the Florida high-school shooting started the protest, and it soon gained momentum across social media.

HOT DOG!
Meat-free sausage on the menu

A sausage made mainly from pea protein was one of *Time* magazine's best inventions of the year. The vegan sausage joined Beyond Meat's other plant-based products, including a meat-free burger. The ingredients in the sausage give it the texture and taste of a meat sausage, with far less fat and no harm to animals. Restaurants and fast-food chains were quick to add the alternative meat to their menus.

STATE WITH
THE OLDEST

Mardi Gras
celebration

ALABAMA

French settlers held the first American Mardi Gras in Mobile, Alabama, in 1703. Yearly celebrations continued until the Civil War and began again in 1866. Today 800,000 people gather in the city during the vibrant two-week festival. Dozens of parades with colorful floats and marching bands wind through the streets each day. Partygoers attend masked balls and other lively events sponsored by the city's social societies. On Mardi Gras, which means "Fat Tuesday" in French, six parades continue the party until the stroke of midnight, which marks the end of the year's festivities and the beginning of Lent.

STATE WITH THE MOST
pilots per capita
ALASKA

Alaska is the only state in the United States in which more than 1 percent of citizens have a pilot's license—no surprise, considering Alaska has many islands and is the largest and most sparsely populated state. If you think this means the state has a surplus of skilled aviators, think again: Despite having six times the national average of pilots per capita, newspapers reported in 2016 that a pilot shortage in Alaska led the state to consider turning to drone technology. Many of its pilots and mechanics leave the state for high-flying careers in the lower forty-eight states.

MOST PILOTS PER CAPITA
Number of pilots per 100 people

Alaska: 1.278

North Dakota: 0.476

Montana: 0.44

Colorado: 0.43

Wyoming: 0.37

STATE WITH THE BEST-PRESERVED
meteor crater
ARIZONA

Fifty thousand years ago, a meteor traveling at 26,000 miles per hour struck the earth near present-day Winslow, Arizona, to create a mile-wide, 550-foot-deep crater. Today, Meteor Crater is a popular tourist destination and is overseen by stewards who work to educate visitors about its formation. There is even an animated movie showing how it happened. The crater is sometimes known as the Barringer Crater, in recognition of mining engineer Daniel Moreau Barringer, who was the one to propose that it had been made by a meteorite. Previously, geologists had believed that the crater was a natural landform created over time.

ONLY STATE WHERE
diamonds are mined
ARKANSAS

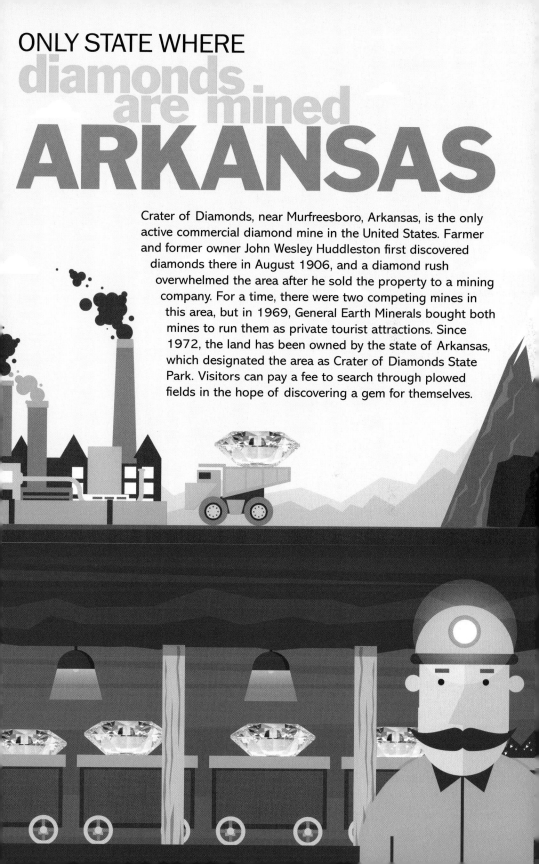

Crater of Diamonds, near Murfreesboro, Arkansas, is the only active commercial diamond mine in the United States. Farmer and former owner John Wesley Huddleston first discovered diamonds there in August 1906, and a diamond rush overwhelmed the area after he sold the property to a mining company. For a time, there were two competing mines in this area, but in 1969, General Earth Minerals bought both mines to run them as private tourist attractions. Since 1972, the land has been owned by the state of Arkansas, which designated the area as Crater of Diamonds State Park. Visitors can pay a fee to search through plowed fields in the hope of discovering a gem for themselves.

MOST DEVOTED
theme-park fan
CALIFORNIA

On June 22, 2017, forty-four-year-old Jeff Reitz completed two thousand consecutive daily visits to the Disneyland and California Adventure Park in Anaheim, California. After finding himself unemployed, the air force veteran bought an annual pass to the theme park in a bid to cheer himself up. That was on January 1, 2012, and Jeff has visited the park every single day since then. These days, having found work, Jeff visits mostly in the evenings. When asked why he keeps coming back, he says it's all about enjoying the magic of the park. His favorite ride is the Matterhorn, a mountain-themed roller coaster on which passengers ride the rails in bobsleds.

STATE WITH THE LARGEST
elk population
COLORADO

Colorado is currently home to around 280,000 elk, making it the state with the largest elk population. Elk live on both public and private land across the state, from the mountainous regions to lower terrain. Popular targets for hunting, these creatures are regulated by both the Colorado Parks and Wildlife department and the National Park Service. Many elk live within the boundaries of Colorado's Rocky Mountain National Park. Elk are among the largest members of the deer family, and the males—called bulls—are distinguishable by their majestic antlers.

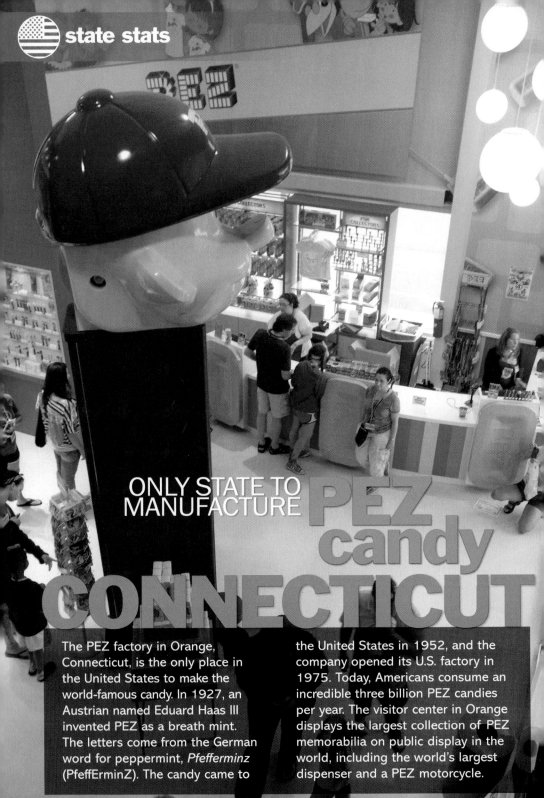

ONLY STATE TO MANUFACTURE PEZ candy CONNECTICUT

The PEZ factory in Orange, Connecticut, is the only place in the United States to make the world-famous candy. In 1927, an Austrian named Eduard Haas III invented PEZ as a breath mint. The letters come from the German word for peppermint, *Pfefferminz* (PfeffErminZ). The candy came to the United States in 1952, and the company opened its U.S. factory in 1975. Today, Americans consume an incredible three billion PEZ candies per year. The visitor center in Orange displays the largest collection of PEZ memorabilia on public display in the world, including the world's largest dispenser and a PEZ motorcycle.

STATE WITH THE MOST
horseshoe crabs
DELAWARE

Delaware Bay has the largest American horseshoe crab (*Limulus polyphemus*) population in the world. These creatures can be seen in large numbers on the bay's beaches in the spring. They appear during high tides on new and full moons, when they come onto land to spawn (deposit eggs). Horseshoe crabs—which are not actually related to other species of crab—have changed very little in the past 250 million years, and have therefore been called "living fossils." It is impossible to know the exact number of horseshoe crabs in the region, so every spring, volunteers at some of the state's beaches conduct counts to track spawning activity. In 2018, the Delaware Center for the Inland Bays reported a count of 16,491 horseshoe crabs across five beaches.

STATE WITH THE MOST-VISITED
amusement park
FLORIDA

Walt Disney World, in Lake Buena Vista, Florida, is home to several parks, including Magic Kingdom, the most-visited amusement park in the United States. Disney parks dominate the most-visited list, taking four of the top five spots. Magic Kingdom sees just over twenty million visitors from around the world who travel each year to ride the attractions, watch parades, and meet their favorite Disney characters. Divided into six themed areas, arguably the most iconic part of the park is Cinderella's Castle, which is illuminated each night by an impressive fireworks display and light-projection show.

MOST VISITED AMUSEMENT PARKS
Number of visitors per year in millions

Magic Kingdom, Walt Disney World, Florida: 20.5

Disneyland, California: 18.3

Tokyo Disneyland, Japan: 16.6

Universal Studios, Japan: 14.9

Tokyo DisneySea, Japan: 13.5

STATE WITH THE LARGEST
Sports Hall of Fame
GEORGIA

At 43,000 square feet, Georgia's Sports Hall of Fame honors the state's greatest sports stars and coaches. The museum includes 14,000 square feet of exhibition space and a 205-seat theater. It owns more than 3,000 artifacts and memorabilia from Georgia's professional, college, and amateur athletes. At least 1,000 of these artifacts are on display at any time. The Hall of Fame corridor features over 300 inductees, such as golf legend Bobby Jones, baseball hero Jackie Robinson, and Olympic track medalist Wyomia Tyus.

ONLY STATE WITH
a royal palace
HAWAII

Iolani Palace, in downtown Honolulu, is the only official royal residence in the United States. The palace was built from 1879–1882 by King Kalakaua, inspired by the styles of the grand castles of Europe. The monarchs did not live there for long, however: In 1893, the kingdom of Hawaii was overthrown by U.S. forces.

Kalakaua's sister, Queen Liliuokalani, was even held prisoner in the palace in 1895 following a plot to put her back on the throne. Iolani Palace was used as a government building until it became a National Historic Landmark in 1962. Restored to its nineteenth-century condition, it is now open to the public as a museum.

FIRST STATE WITH a blue football field

Boise State's Albertsons Stadium, originally dubbed the "Smurf Turf" and now nicknamed "The Blue," was the first blue football field in the United States. In 1986, when the time came to upgrade the old turf, athletics director Gene Bleymaier realized that they would be spending a lot of money on the new field, yet most spectators wouldn't notice the difference. So, he asked AstroTurf to create the new field in the school's colors. Since the field's creation, students at the school have consistently voted for blue turf each time the field has been upgraded. Today, five more teams have opted for a colored playing field, including Eastern Washington, whose red field is dubbed "The Inferno," and Central Arkansas, where the teams play on purple and gray stripes.

IDAHO

STATE WITH THE OLDEST
free public zoo

Lincoln Park Zoo, in Chicago, Illinois, remains the oldest free public zoo in the United States. Founded in 1868—nine years after the Philadelphia Zoo, the country's oldest zoo overall—Lincoln Park Zoo does not charge admission fees. More than two-thirds of the money for the zoo's operating budget comes from food, retail, parking, and fund-raising events. Nonetheless, the zoo continues to grow. In November 2016, it opened a new exhibit—the Walter Family Arctic Tundra—to house its newest addition: a seven-year-old male polar bear named Siku.

ILLINOIS

THE FIRST
professional baseball game

INDIANA

On May 4, 1871, the first National Association professional baseball game took place on Hamilton Field at Fort Wayne, Indiana. The home team, the Kekiongas, took on Forest City of Cleveland, beating them 2–0 against the odds. The Kekiongas were a little-known team at the time. In fact, this first game had been scheduled to take place between better-known Washington Olympic Club and the Cincinnati Red Stockings in Washington, D.C., on May 3. Heavy rain forced a cancellation, however, and so history was made at Fort Wayne the following day.

STATE WITH THE SHORTEST, STEEPEST
railroad
IOWA

At only 296 feet long, Fenelon Place Elevator in Dubuque, Iowa, is the shortest railroad in the United States, and its elevation of 189 feet also makes it the steepest. The original railway was built in 1882 by businessman and former mayor J. K. Graves, who lived at the top of the Mississippi River bluff and wanted a quicker commute down into the town below. Today's railway, modernized in 1977, is open to the public. It costs $1.50 for an adult one-way trip and consists of two quaint house-shaped cars traveling in opposite directions on parallel tracks.

STATE WITH THE MOST
rock concretions

Rock City, in Minneapolis, Kansas, boasts two hundred concretions of Dakota sandstone across a 5-acre park. They are the largest concretions in one place anywhere in the world. These concretions are huge spheres of rock, some of which measure up to 27 feet in diameter. They were created underground millions of years ago, when minerals deposited by water gradually formed hard, strong shells around small bits of matter in the sandstone. Over time, as the surrounding sandstone wore down, the concretions survived. Today, Rock City is a registered National Natural Landmark, and visitors can explore the park and climb the concretions for a $3.00 fee.

KANSAS

KENTUCKY

STATE WITH THE BIGGEST
fireworks display

The Kentucky Derby is the longest-running sporting event in the United States and proudly claims to be the "most exciting two minutes in sport." It's also accompanied by the biggest fireworks display held annually in the United States—"Thunder Over Louisville"—which kicks off the racing festivities. Zambelli Fireworks, which creates the display, says that the show requires nearly 60 tons of fireworks shells and a massive 700 miles of wire cable to sync the fireworks to music. The theme for the 2019 firework display was "The Wonderful World of Thunder."

STATE WITH THE MOST
crawfish
LOUISIANA

The majority of the crawfish consumed in the United States are caught in the state of Louisiana. While these critters may look like tiny lobsters, crawfish are actually freshwater shellfish and are abundant in the mud of the state's bayous— sometimes they are called "mudbugs." Before white settlers arrived in Louisiana, crawfish were a favorite food of the native tribes, who caught them using reeds baited with venison. Today, crawfish are both commercially farmed and caught in their natural habitat. The industry yields between 120 and 150 million pounds of crawfish a year, and the crustaceans are an integral part of the state's culture, with backyard crawfish boils remaining a popular local tradition.

state with the oldest state fair

MAINE

SKOWHEGAN
STATE FAIR 1880

In January 1819, the Somerset Central Agricultural Society sponsored the first-ever Skowhegan State Fair. In the 1800s, state fairs were important places for farmers to gather and learn about new agricultural methods and equipment. After Maine became a state in 1820, the fair continued to grow in size and popularity, gaining its official name in 1842. Today, the Skowhegan State Fair welcomes more than 7,000 exhibitors and 100,000 visitors. Enthusiasts can watch events that include livestock competitions, tractor pulling, a demolition derby, and much more during the ten-day show.

STATE WITH THE OLDEST
capitol building
MARYLAND

The Maryland State House in Annapolis is both the oldest capitol building in continuous legislative use and the only state house once to have been used as the national capitol. The Continental Congress met there from 1783–1784, and it was where George Washington formally resigned as commander in chief of the army following the American Revolution. The current building is the third to be erected on that site, and was actually incomplete when the Continental Congress met there in 1783, despite the cornerstone being laid in 1772. The interior of the building was finished in 1797, but not without tragedy—plasterer Thomas Dance fell to his death while working on the dome in 1793.

OLDEST CAPITOL BUILDINGS IN 2019
Age of building (year work was started)

Maryland: 247 years (1772)

Virginia: 234 years (1785)

New Jersey: 227 years (1792)

Massachusetts: 224 years (1795)

New Hampshire: 203 years (1816)

MASSACHUSETTS

STATE WITH
THE OLDEST
Thanksgiving
celebration

The first Thanksgiving celebration took place in 1621, in Plymouth, Massachusetts, when the Pilgrims held a feast to celebrate the harvest. They shared their meal with the native Wampanoag people from a nearby village. While the celebration became widespread in the Northeast in the late seventeenth century,

Thanksgiving was not celebrated nationally until 1863, when magazine editor Sarah Josepha Hale's writings convinced President Abraham Lincoln to make it a national holiday. Today, Plymouth, Massachusetts, holds a weekend-long celebration honoring its history: the America's Hometown Thanksgiving Celebration.

MOST MAGICAL state
MICHIGAN

Colon, Michigan, is known as the magic capital of the world. The small town is home to Abbott Magic Company—one of the biggest manufacturers of magic supplies in the United States—as well as an annual magic festival, magicians' walk of fame, and Colon Lakeside Cemetery, in which twenty-eight magicians are buried. The Abbott plant boasts 50,000 square feet dedicated to creating new tricks— from simple silk scarves to custom illusions. It is the only building in the world expressly built for the purpose of making magic.

STATE WITH THE LARGEST mall

MINNESOTA

The biggest shopping and entertainment center in the United States is the Mall of America in Bloomington, Minnesota. Spread over 5.4 million square feet with 12,000 parking spaces, it attracts forty million people a year. As well as the 500 retail units, the mall also contains the Nickelodeon Universe indoor amusement park and an aquarium. Minnesota is also considered the birthplace of the modern shopping mall as it is home to Southdale Center in Edina, one of the first malls, which opened in 1956.

MISSISSIPPI

only state to hold the International Ballet Competition

Every four years, Jackson, Mississippi, hosts the USA International Ballet Competition, a two-week Olympic-style event that awards gold, silver, and bronze medals. The competition began in 1964 in Varna, Bulgaria, and rotated among the cities of Varna; Moscow, Russia; and Tokyo, Japan. In June 1979, the competition came to the United States for the first time, and, in 1982, Congress passed a Joint Resolution designating Jackson as the official home of the competition. In addition to medals, dancers vie for cash prizes and the chance to join established ballet companies.

America's first ice-cream cone

MISSOURI

It is said that America's first ice-cream cone was introduced through chance inspiration at the St. Louis World's Fair in 1904. According to the most popular story, a Syrian salesman named Ernest Hamwi saw that an ice-cream vendor had plenty of ice cream but not enough cups and spoons to serve it. Seeing that a neighboring vendor was selling waffle cookies, Hamwi took a cookie and rolled it into a cone for holding ice cream. An immediate success, Hamwi's invention was hailed by vendors as a "cornucopia"—an exotic word for a "cone."

STATE WITH THE MOST
T. rex specimens

The first *Tyrannosaurus rex* fossil ever found was discovered in Montana—paleontologist Barnum Brown excavated it in the Hell Creek Formation in 1902. Since then, many major T. rex finds have been in Montana—from the "Wankel Rex," discovered in 1988, to "Trix," discovered in 2013.

Another T. rex fossil was uncovered in Montana in 2016: "Tufts-Love Rex," named for paleontologists Jason Love and Luke Tufts, was found about 20 percent intact at the site in Hell Creek. Today, the Museum of the Rockies in Bozeman, Montana, houses thirteen T. rex specimens—more than anywhere else in the world.

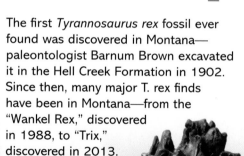

MONTANA

STATE WITH THE LARGEST
indoor rain forest

NEBRASKA

The Lied Jungle at Henry Doorly Zoo in Omaha, Nebraska, features three rain-forest habitats: one each from South America, Africa, and Asia. At 123,000 square feet, this indoor rain forest is larger than two football fields. It measures 80 feet tall, making it as tall as an eight-story building. The Lied Jungle opened in 1992 and cost $15 million to create.

Seven waterfalls rank among its spectacular features. Ninety different animal species live here, including saki monkeys, pygmy hippos, and many reptiles and birds. Exotic plant life includes the African sausage tree, the chocolate tree, and rare orchids. The zoo's other major exhibit—the Desert Dome—is the world's largest indoor desert.

STATE THAT PRODUCES the most gold
NEVADA

Although it has been called the "Silver State" for its silver production, Nevada is also the state that produces the most gold. According to the Nevada Mining Association, Nevada produces more than three-quarters of America's gold and accounts for 5.4 percent of world gold production. Gold can be found in every county of Nevada, although it is not always accessible to casual prospectors. Nevada's Carlin Trend is rich in gold deposits—and is, in fact, the world's second-largest gold resource—but the deposits are so finely spread that they require an expensive process to extract the precious mineral.

STATE WITH THE OLDEST skiing club

NEW HAMPSHIRE

Nansen Ski Club, in Milan, New Hampshire, was founded by Norwegian immigrants in 1872, making it the oldest continuously operating skiing club in the United States. When it first opened, the venue only accepted other Scandinavians living in the area, but was then made available to everyone as more skiing enthusiasts began to move into New Hampshire from Quebec, to work in the mills there. For fifty years, the club was home to the largest ski jump east of the Mississippi, and was used for Olympic tryouts.

STATE WITH THE MOST
diners

NEW JERSEY

The state of New Jersey has more than six hundred diners, earning it the title of "Diner Capital of the World." The state has a higher concentration of diners than anywhere else in the United States. They are such an iconic part of the state's identity that, in 2016, a New Jersey diners exhibit opened at Middlesex County Museum, showcasing the history of the diner from early twentieth-century lunch cars to modern roadside spots. The state has many different types of diners, including famous restaurant-style eateries like Tops in East Newark, as well as retro hole-in-the-wall diners with jukeboxes and faded booths.

STATE THAT MADE THE WORLD'S LARGEST
flat enchilada

New Mexico was home to the world's largest flat enchilada in October 2014, during the Whole Enchilada Fiesta in Las Cruces. The record-breaking enchilada measured 10.5 feet in diameter and required 250 pounds of masa dough, 175 pounds of cheese, 75 gallons of red chili sauce, 50 pounds of onions, and 175 gallons of oil. Led by Roberto's Mexican Restaurant, the making—and eating—of the giant enchilada was a tradition at the festival for thirty-four years before enchilada master Roberto Estrada hung up his apron in 2015.

NEW MEXICO

America's smallest church

NEW YORK

The smallest church in America, Oneida's Cross Island Chapel, measures 81 by 51 inches and has just enough room for the minister and two churchgoers. Built in 1989, the church is in an odd location, in the middle of a pond. The simple, whitewashed clapboard chapel stands on a little jetty that has moorings for a boat or two. The island that the chapel is named for barely breaks the surface of the water nearby and is simply a craggy pile of rock bearing a cross.

STATE WITH
THE LARGEST
private house
NORTH
CAROLINA

The Biltmore Estate, in the mountains of Asheville, North Carolina, is home to Biltmore House, the largest privately owned house in the United States. George Vanderbilt commissioned the 250-room French Renaissance–style chateau in 1889, and opened it to his friends and family as a country retreat in 1895. Designed by architect Richard Morris Hunt, Biltmore House has an impressive thirty-five bedrooms and forty-three bathrooms, and boasts a floor space of over four acres. In 1930, the Vanderbilt family opened Biltmore House to the public.

LARGEST PRIVATE HOUSES IN THE USA
Area in square feet

Biltmore House, Asheville, NC: 175,000

Oheka Castle, Huntington, NY: 109,000

Sydell Miller Mansion, Palm Beach, FL: 84,626

Pensmore, Highlandville, MO: 72,215

Rennert Mansion, Sagaponack, NY: 66,400

BIGGEST honey producer NORTH DAKOTA

For the last thirteen years, North Dakota has outstripped all other U.S. states in the production of honey. Currently, there are 485,000 honey-producing colonies in North Dakota, and in 2016, they produced more than 37.8 million pounds of the sweet stuff. It seems the North Dakota climate is just right for honeybees and—more important—for the flowers from which they collect their nectar. Typical summer weather features warm days but cool nights.

NO SELF RESPECTING WOMA

SHOULD WISH OR WORK

FOR THE SUCCE

SUSAN B. ANTHON

FIRST LAWS **protecting working women OHIO**

In the 1800s, working conditions in U.S. factories were grueling and pay was very low. Most of the workers were women, and it was not uncommon for them to work for twelve to fourteen hours a day, six days a week. The factories were not heated or air-conditioned and there was no compensation for being sick.

By the 1850s, several organizations had formed to improve the working conditions for women and to shorten their workday. In 1852, Ohio passed a law limiting the working day to ten hours for women under the age of eighteen. It was a small step, but it was also the first act of legislation of its kind in the United States.

STATE WITH THE LARGEST
multiple-arch dam
OKLAHOMA

Completed in 1940, the Pensacola Dam in Oklahoma is 6,565 feet long, making it the longest multiple-arch dam in the world. The dam stretches across the Grand River and controls the 43,500 acres of water that form the Grand Lake o' the Cherokees.

The massive structure is a towering 145 feet tall and consists of no fewer than 535,000 cubic yards of concrete, about 655,000 barrels of cement, 75,000 pounds of copper, and a weighty 10 million pounds of structural steel.

STATE WITH THE MOST
photographed
lighthouse
OREGON

Halfway between the towns of Florence and Yachats, Oregon's Heceta Head Lighthouse is the most photographed lighthouse in the United States. Built around 1894, the 205-foot-tall lighthouse is on the National Register of Historic Places, and while the light still works, it is now better known as a romantic bed-and-breakfast location. Heceta Head Lighthouse is famous not just for its beauty—it is also considered one of America's most haunted lighthouses, with stories claiming it is home to a "Gray Lady" called Rue.

STATE THAT MANUFACTURES
the most crayons

PENNSYLVANIA

Easton, Pennsylvania, is home to the Crayola crayon factory and has been the company's headquarters since 1976. The factory produces an amazing twelve million crayons every single day, made from uncolored paraffin and pigment powder.

In 1996, the company opened the Crayola Experience in downtown Easton. The Experience includes a live interactive show in which guests can watch a "crayonologist" make crayons, just as they are made at the factory nearby.

STATE WITH THE OLDEST
Fourth of July celebration

RHODE ISLAND

Bristol, Rhode Island, holds America's longest continuously running Fourth of July celebration. The idea for the celebration came from Revolutionary War veteran Rev. Henry Wight, of Bristol's First Congregational Church, who organized "Patriotic Exercises" to honor the nation's founders and those who fought to establish the United States. Today, Bristol begins celebrating the holiday on June 14, and puts on a wide array of events leading up to the Fourth itself—including free concerts, a baseball game, a Fourth of July Ball, and a half marathon.

STATE WITH THE HOTTEST pepper

SOUTH CAROLINA

Pepper X, created by Smokin' Ed Currie of Rock Hill, South Carolina, is the hottest pepper in the world, measuring an average of 3.18 million Scoville heat units (SHU). To get a feel for how hot that is, just know that a regular jalapeño clocks in at 10,000 to 20,000 SHU. Currie also created the world's third-hottest chili, the Carolina Reaper. The Reaper held the record from 2013 to 2017, before being beaten by the 2.4 million SHU Dragon's Breath pepper in May. Just four months after that, Currie's Pepper X took the chili pepper world by storm.

WORLD'S HOTTEST PEPPERS
By peak heat in millions of SHU

Pepper X: 3.18

Dragon's Breath: 2.4

Carolina Reaper: 2.2

Trinidad Moruga Scorpion: 2

Brain Strain: 1.9

STATE WITH THE LARGEST
sculpture
SOUTH DAKOTA

While South Dakota is famous as the home of Mount Rushmore, it is also the location of another giant mountain carving: the Crazy Horse Memorial. The mountain carving, which is still in progress, will be the largest sculpture in the world when it is completed, at 563 feet tall and 641 feet long. Korczak Ziolkowski, who worked on Mount Rushmore, began the carving in 1948 to pay tribute to Crazy Horse—the Lakota Sioux leader who defeated General Custer at the Battle of the Little Bighorn. Nearly seventy years later, Ziolkowski's family continues his work, relying completely on funding from visitors and donors.

STATE THAT MAKES ALL THE
MoonPies
TENNESSEE

Tennessee is the home of the MoonPie, which was conceived there in 1917 by bakery salesman Earl Mitchell Sr. after a group of local miners asked for a filling treat "as big as the moon." Made from marshmallow, graham crackers, and chocolate, the sandwich cookies were soon being mass-produced at Tennessee's Chattanooga Bakery, and MoonPie was registered as a trademark by the bakery in 1919. MoonPies first sold at just five cents each and quickly became popular—even being named the official snack of NASCAR in the late 1990s. Today, Chattanooga Bakery makes nearly a million MoonPies every day.

LARGEST
urban bat
colony
TEXAS

If you want to see a sky filled with hundreds of thousands of bats, head to Austin, Texas, any time from mid-March to November. The city's Ann W. Richards Congress Avenue Bridge is home to the world's largest urban bat colony—roughly 1.5 million bats in all. The Mexican free-tailed bats first settled here in the 1980s, and numbers have grown steadily since. They currently produce around 750,000 pups per year. These days the bats are a tourist attraction that draws about 140,000 visitors to the city, many of them hoping to catch the moment at dusk when large numbers of bats fly out from under the bridge to look for food.

STATE WITH THE LARGEST
saltwater lake
UTAH

The Great Salt Lake, which inspired the name of Utah's largest city, is the largest saltwater lake in the United States, at around 75 miles long and 35 miles wide. Sometimes called "America's Dead Sea," it is typically larger than each of the states of Delaware and Rhode Island. Its size, however, fluctuates as water levels rise and fall: Since 1849, the water level has varied by as much as 20 feet, which can shift the shoreline by up to 15 miles. Great Salt Lake is too salty to support most aquatic life but is home to several kinds of algae as well as the brine shrimp that feed on them.

STATE THAT PRODUCES THE MOST

maple syrup

VERMONT

The state of Vermont produced 1.94 million gallons of maple syrup in 2018, contributing more than 46 percent of the national total. Vermont's more than 1,500 maple syrup producers take sap from 5.67 million tree taps. They have to collect 40 gallons of maple sap in order to produce just 1 gallon of syrup. Producers also use maple sap for making other treats, such as maple butter, sugar, and candies.

STATE WITH THE LARGEST
office building
VIRGINIA

The Pentagon—the headquarters of the United States Department of Defense—is America's largest office building. The five-sided structure, which was completed in 1943 after just sixteen months of work, cost $83 million to build. It contains 3.7 million square feet of office space—and triple the amount of floor space in the Empire State Building—as well as a large central courtyard. Despite containing 17.5 miles of corridors, the building's design means that a person can walk from any point to another in about 7 minutes. There are currently 24,000 employees, both military and civilian, working in the building.

The Teapot Dome Service Station in Zillah, Washington, was once the oldest working gas station in the United States, and is still the only one built to commemorate a political scandal. Now preserved as a museum, the gas station was built in 1922 as a monument to the Teapot Dome Scandal, in which Albert Fall, President Warren G. Harding's secretary of the interior, took bribes to lease government oil reserves to private companies. The gas station, located on Washington's Old Highway 12, was moved in 1978 to make way for Interstate 82, then again in 2007 when it was purchased by the City of Zillah as a historic landmark.

STATE WITH THE OLDEST gas station
WASHINGTON

STATE WITH THE LONGEST steel arch bridge
WEST bridge
VIRGINIA

The New River Gorge Bridge in Fayetteville spans 3,030 feet and is 876 feet above the New River. It is both the longest and largest steel arch bridge in the United States. Builders used 88 million pounds of steel and concrete to construct it. The $37 million structure took three years to complete and opened on October 22, 1977. Bridge Day, held every October since 1980, is a BASE-jumping event at the New River Gorge Bridge. Hundreds of BASE jumpers and about 80,000 spectators gather for the one-day festival. Among the most popular events is the Big Way, in which large groups of people jump off the bridge together. During Bridge Day 2013, Donald Cripps became one of the world's oldest BASE jumpers, at eighty-four years old.

LARGEST

cross-country
ski race
WISCONSIN

Each year in February, Wisconsin hosts America's largest cross-country ski race. The race attracts over 10,000 skiers, all attempting to complete the 55-kilometer (34-mile) course from Cable to Hayward. Milestones along the way include Boedecker Hill, Mosquito Brook, and Hatchery Park.

The event is part of the Worldloppet circuit of twenty ski marathons across the globe. The winner of the 2018 race, Benjamin Saxton from Lakeville, Minnesota, completed the course in two hours, forty-seven minutes, and thirty-five seconds to claim the $7,500 prize money.

STATE WITH THE LARGEST
hot spring
WYOMING

Grand Prismatic Spring, in Yellowstone National Park in Wyoming, is the largest hot spring in the United States. The spring measures 370 feet in diameter and is more than 121 feet deep; Yellowstone National Park says that the spring is bigger than a football field and deeper than a ten-story building. Grand Prismatic is not just the largest spring but also the most photographed thermal feature in Yellowstone due to its bright colors. The colors come from different kinds of bacteria, living in each part of the spring, that thrive at various temperatures. As water comes up from the middle of the spring, it is too hot to support most bacterial life, but as the water spreads out to the edges of the spring, it cools in concentric circles.

sports STARS

SPORTS STARS
TRENDING

PERFECT 10
Gymnast wows the Internet

A video of Katelyn Ohashi's gymnastic floor routine won her nine million views in twenty-four hours. The video followed Ohashi's triumph at the Collegiate Challenge, where the judges awarded her a perfect score of ten. Ohashi's energetic performance featured a series of sensational jumps, flips, and splits. The UCLA student was twelve years old when she made the Junior National Team.

HIP-HOP ON ICE
Skater's daring music choice

Skater Ma got the Internet buzzing after his routine at the United States Figure Skating Championships. Ma finished in eleventh place in the competition, but the reason for the social media frenzy was Ma's unusual music choice. Instead of a standard classical or jazz piece, the twenty-two-year old skater used a remix of electronic hip-hop songs, "Turn Down for What" by DJ Snake and Lil Jon and "Propaganda" by DJ Snake.

SPINNING BUMBLEBEE
Break dancing at the Youth Olympics

For the first time, break dancing became an Olympic sport when it was introduced at the 2018 Youth Olympics. Russian athlete Sergei Chernyshev, who goes by the nickname "Bumblebee," won gold in the boys' competition, and Ramu "Ram" Kawai earned a gold medal for the girls' event. Paris is considering a proposal to include break dancing, or simply "breaking," in the 2024 Olympics.

TEARS OF JOY
Football star reaches out to one-handed athlete

Shaquem Griffin, a player for the Seattle Seahawks, brought an eleven-year-old fan to happy tears. Griffin sent a jersey to Daniel for his birthday, and the video of the young fan's joyful, but tearful, reaction went viral. Both Griffin, a professional athlete, and Daniel, a young football player, have one hand. Griffin followed the gift by sending a happy birthday video to Daniel, and an invitation to meet and attend a Seahawks game.

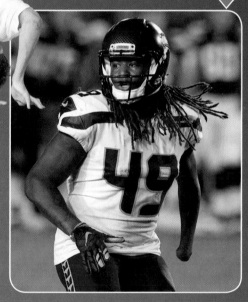

TWITTER GOLD
Olympic boarder tweets between runs

Chloe Kim won a gold medal and thousands of Twitter followers at the 2018 Winter Olympics. Twitter lit up as Kim tweeted between runs while competing in the women's halfpipe.

During the nail-biting qualifiers, Kim tweeted about wanting an ice cream. Just before her last run, which earned her a score of 98.25, Kim pulled out her phone to tweet about not finishing her breakfast sandwich. After winning the gold, Kim's Twitter followers had jumped from 15,000 to over 100,000.

WORLD'S HIGHEST BASE jump from a building

FRED FUGEN AND VINCE REFFET

BASE jumping is just about the world's most terrifying sport to watch. BASE stands for the types of places a person may jump from: Buildings, Antennae, Spans (usually bridges), and Earth (usually cliffs). In April 2014, French daredevils Fred Fugen and Vince Reffet set a new record by jumping from a specially built platform at the top of the world's tallest building, the Burj Khalifa in Dubai. They jumped from a height of 2,716 feet 6 inches. The highest ever BASE jump was performed by Russian Valery Rozov from 23,690 feet high on the north side of Mount Everest. He landed safely on the Rongbuk Glacier at an altitude of 19,520 feet, some 4,100 feet below.

WORLD'S HIGHEST
tightrope walk
FREDDY NOCK

Tightrope walking looks hard enough a few feet above the ground, but Swiss stuntman Freddy Nock took it to the next level when he walked between two mountains in the Swiss Alps in March 2015. On a rope set 11,590 feet above sea level, Freddy took about thirty-nine minutes to walk the 1,140 feet across to the neighboring peak. The previous record had held since 1974, when Frenchman Philippe Petit walked between the Twin Towers of New York's former World Trade Center.

WORLD'S LONGEST
skateboard
ramp jump
DANNY
WAY

Many extreme sports activities are showcased at the annual X Games and Winter X Games. At the 2004 X Games, held in Los Angeles, skateboarder Danny Way set an amazing record that remains unbeaten. On June 19, Way made a long-distance jump of 79 feet, beating his own 2003 world record (75 feet). In 2005 he jumped over the Great Wall of China. He made the jump despite having torn ligaments in his ankle during a practice jump on the previous day.

JOCKEY WITH THE MOST
Triple Crown wins

EDDIE ARCARO

Many horse-racing experts think that Eddie Arcaro was the best-ever American jockey. Arcaro rode his first winner in 1932, and by the time of his retirement thirty years later, he had won the Triple Crown twice, in 1941 and 1948. He also won more Triple Crown races than any other jockey, although Bill Hartack has equaled Arcaro's total of five successes in the Kentucky Derby. Arcaro won 4,779 races overall in his career.

JOCKEYS WITH MULTIPLE WINS IN TRIPLE CROWN RACES
Number of wins (years active)

Eddie Arcaro	17	1938–1957
Bill Shoemaker	11	1955–1986
Earl Sande	9	1921–1930
Bill Hartack	9	1956–1969
Pat Day	9	1985–2000
Gary Stevens	9	1988–2013

WORLD'S HIGHEST basketball shot

HOW RIDICULOUS

Australian trick-shot group How Ridiculous continues to break its own record. In 2015 one member made a basket from an amazing 415 feet, but the group has since improved that distance several times. In January 2018 How Ridiculous achieved its most astonishing feat yet: a basket from 660 feet, 10 inches. The group made the record shot at Maletsunyane Falls, Lesotho, in southern Africa, after five days of setup work and practice. How Ridiculous is a group of three friends who started trying trick shots for fun in their backyards in 2009. They now have a successful YouTube channel and business and are also involved in Christian charitable work.

268

NBA team

WITH THE MOST CHAMPIONSHIP TITLES

BOSTON CELTICS

The Boston Celtics top the NBA winners' list with seventeen championship titles out of twenty-one appearances in the finals, just one title more than the Los Angeles Lakers. The two teams have met twelve times in the finals, resulting in nine wins for the Celtics. The best years for the Boston Celtics were the 1960s, with 1967 being the only year in the decade that they did not bring the championship home.

NBA CHAMPIONSHIP WINS

Boston Celtics	17	1957–2008
LA Lakers	16	1949–2010
Golden State Warriors	6	1947–2018
Chicago Bulls	6	1991–1998
San Antonio Spurs	5	1999–2014

MOST CAREER POINTS
in the
NBA
KAREEM
ABDUL-JABBAR

Many fans regard Abdul-Jabbar as the greatest-ever basketball player. Abdul-Jabbar was known by his birth name, Lew Alcindor, until 1971, when he changed his name after converting to Islam. That same year he led the Milwaukee Bucks to the team's first NBA championship title. As well as being the all-time highest scorer of points during his professional career with a total of 38,387, Abdul-Jabbar also won the NBA Most Valuable Player (MVP) award a record six times.

NBA MOST CAREER POINTS LEADERS
Number of points

Kareem Abdul-Jabbar	38,387
Karl Malone	36,928
Kobe Bryant	33,643
LeBron James	32,543
Michael Jordan	32,292

YOUNGEST NBA PLAYER
to reach 30,000 career points
LEBRON JAMES

On Tuesday, January 23, 2018, at the age of thirty-three years and twenty-four days, LeBron James became the youngest player in NBA history to reach 30,000 points, smashing Kobe Bryant's previous record by more than a year. On top of building his own scoring record, James also works hard for his team. In February 2019, James made NBA history again, becoming the youngest player to reach 32,000 points. James may even challenge Kareem Abdul-Jabbar in the career-points table before he retires.

DIANA TAURASI

WNBA PLAYER WITH THE MOST
career points

MOST CAREER POINTS IN THE WNBA
Number of points

Diana Taurasi	8,549
Tina Thompson	7,488
Tamika Catchings	7,380
Cappie Pondexter	6,811
Katie Smith	6,452

After a standout college career and three NCAA championships with the University of Connecticut Huskies, Diana Taurasi joined the Phoenix Mercury in the WNBA in 2004. Her prolific scoring helped the Mercury to their first WNBA title in 2007 (and two more since then) and her international career includes four consecutive Team USA Olympic golds, 2004–16. Playing mainly as guard, Taurasi became the all-time leading WNBA scorer in 2017.

football team
DALLAS COWBOYS

It has been more than twenty years since the Dallas Cowboys won the Super Bowl, yet the team has been the most valuable in the NFL for twelve straight seasons up to 2018. The team was most recently valued at $5 billion. Cowboys' owner Jerry Jones paid what now seems a bargain $150 million for the franchise in 1989. In recent years broadcast and stadium revenues in the NFL have soared.

NFL TEAM VALUATIONS
Revenue in billions of U.S. dollars
September 2017

Dallas Cowboys	5.0
New England Patriots	3.8
New York Giants	3.3
Los Angeles Rams	3.3
Washington Redskins	3.1

NFL PLAYER
WITH THE
MOST

career touchdowns
JERRY RICE

Jerry Rice is generally regarded as the greatest wide receiver in NFL history. He played in the NFL for twenty seasons—fifteen of them with the San Francisco 49ers—and won three Super Bowl rings. As well as leading the career touchdowns list with 208, Rice also holds the "most yards gained" mark with 23,546 yards. Most of his touchdowns were from pass receptions (197), often working with the great 49ers quarterback Joe Montana.

NFL PLAYERS WITH THE MOST CAREER TOUCHDOWNS
Number of touchdowns (career years)

Jerry Rice	208	1985–2004
Emmitt Smith	175	1990–2004
LaDainian Tomlinson	162	2001–2011
Terrell Owens	156	1996–2010
Randy Moss	156	1998–2012

DREW BREES

Drew Brees is one of the greatest quarterbacks of all time. After a stellar college career at Purdue he spent five seasons with the Chargers before joining the New Orleans Saints in 2006. He was still starring with the Saints in the 2018 season, only just missing out on leading them to the Super Bowl after a controversial refereeing decision in the NFC championship clash with the Rams. As well as total pass completions, Brees holds NFL records for career passing yards and completion percentage and was named MVP in the Saints' Super Bowl XLIV triumph.

NFL PLAYERS WITH THE MOST CAREER TOUCHDOWNS
Number of touchdowns (career years)

Drew Brees	6,586	2001–2018
Brett Favre	6,300	1991–2010
Peyton Manning	6,125	1998–2015
Tom Brady	6,004	2000–2018
Dan Marino	4,967	1983–1999

NFL TEAM WITH THE MOST
Super Bowl appearances

Founded in 1959 as one of the members of the new American Football League, the then-Boston Patriots struggled for many years. They only made their first Super Bowl appearance in 1985, when they lost to the Bears, but in recent years they have been the NFL's dominant force. Led by veteran quarterback Tom Brady and coach Bill Belichik, they have played in four out of five Super Bowls, 2014–18, and won three of them. They are now tied with the Steelers for most Super Bowl successes but well ahead of all the others with eleven appearances in total.

NEW ENGLAND PATRIOTS

NFL TEAMS WITH THE MOST SUPER BOWL WINS
Number of wins

Team	Number of wins	Super Bowls
New England Patriots	6	Super Bowls XXXVI, XXXVIII, XXXIX, XLIX, LI, LIII
Pittsburgh Steelers	6	Super Bowls IX, X, XIII, XIV, XL, XLIII
San Francisco 49ers	5	Super Bowls XVI, XIX, XXIII, XXIV, XXIX
Dallas Cowboys	5	Super Bowls VI, XII, XXVII, XXVIII, XXX
Green Bay Packers	4	Super Bowls I, II, XXXI, XLV
New York Giants	4	Super Bowls XXI, XXV, XLII, XLVI

school with most Rose Bowl wins

The Rose Bowl is college football's oldest postseason event, first played in 1902. Taking place near January 1 of each year, the game is normally played between the Pac-12 Conference champion and the Big Ten Conference champion, but one year in three is part of college football's playoffs.

The University of Southern California has easily the best record in the Rose Bowl, with twenty-five wins from thirty-four appearances, followed by the Michigan Wolverines (eight wins from twenty). The Ohio State Buckeyes defeated the Washington Huskies 28–23 in the 2019 game. The Buckeyes now also have eight Rose Bowl wins.

USC TROJANS

MLB TEAM WITH THE MOST
World Series wins

NEW YORK YANKEES

WORLD SERIES WINS
Number of wins

New York Yankees	27	1923–2009
St. Louis Cardinals	11	1926–2011
Oakland Athletics*	9	1910–1989
San Francisco Giants**	8	1905–2014
Boston Red Sox***	9	1903–2018

* Previously played in Kansas City and Philadelphia

** Previously played in New York

*** Originally Boston Americans

The New York Yankees are far and away the most successful team in World Series history. Since baseball's championship was first contested in 1903, the Yankees have appeared forty times and won on twenty-seven occasions. The Yankees' greatest years were from the 1930s through the 1950s, when the team was led by legends like Babe Ruth and Joe DiMaggio. Nearest challengers are the St. Louis Cardinals from the National League with eleven wins from nineteen appearances.

LONGEST
World Series championship drought

The 2016 World Series saw a dramatic showdown between the two Major League Baseball clubs with the longest World Series droughts: the Chicago Cubs and the Cleveland Indians. The Cubs had been one of baseball's most successful teams in the early years of the World Series at the start of the twentieth century, but between 1908 and 1945, they lost the World Series seven times. Following that string of World Series losses, the team scarcely won even a divisional title until 2016—the year the drought finally ended. The Cubs clinched the World Series title in the tenth inning in the deciding seventh game.

CHICAGO CUBS, BROKEN 2016

WORLD SERIES DROUGHTS

Team	Last World Series win	Last appearance in World Series
Cleveland Indians	1948	2016
Texas Rangers	Never (since 1961*)	2011
Milwaukee Brewers	Never (since 1969*)	1982

MLB PLAYER WITH THE HIGHEST
batting average

HIGHEST CAREER BATTING AVERAGES
Batting average (career years)

Ty Cobb	.366	1905–1928
Rogers Hornsby	.359	1915–1937
Shoeless Joe Jackson	.356	1908–1920
Lefty O'Doul	.349	1919–1934
Ed Delahanty	.346	1888–1903

TY COBB

Ty Cobb's batting average of .366 is one of the longest-lasting records in Major League Baseball. In reaching that mark, Cobb, known to fans as "The Georgia Peach," astonishingly batted .300 or better in twenty-three consecutive seasons, mainly with the Detroit Tigers. Cobb's status in the game was made clear when he easily topped the selection poll for the first set of inductees into the Baseball Hall of Fame.

CAREER HOME RUNS
Number of home runs (career years)

Barry Bonds	762	1986–2007
Hank Aaron	755	1954–1976
Babe Ruth	714	1914–1935
Alex Rodriguez	696	1994–2016
Willie Mays	660	1951–1973

Barry Bonds's power hitting and skill in the outfield rank him as a five-tool player—someone with good speed and baserunning skills, who is also good at hitting the ball, fielding, and throwing. He played his first seven seasons with the Pittsburgh Pirates before moving to the San Francisco Giants for the next twelve seasons. He not only holds the record for most career home runs, but also for the single-season record of seventy-three home runs, which was set in 2001. Barry's godfather is Willie Mays, the first player ever to hit 300 career home runs and steal 300 bases.

BARRY BONDS

BECK.
47

MLS PLAYER WITH THE MOST
regular-season goals

LANDON DONOVAN

Through April 2019, Landon Donovan was Major League Soccer's all-time top scorer. After coming out of retirement for the 2016 season Donovan took his total to 145 regular-season goals and 136 assists. In addition, Donovan held the goal-scoring record for the U.S. national team, with 57 from 157 appearances. Donovan played for LA Galaxy for most of his career, but also appeared and scored in the German Bundesliga and the English Premier League.

MLS REGULAR-SEASON TOP SCORERS
Number of goals (career years)

Player	Goals	Years
Landon Donovan	145	2001–2016
Chris Wondolowski	144	2005–
Jeff Cunningham	134	1998–2011
Jaime Moreno	133	1996–2010
Ante Razov	114	1996–2009

COUNTRY WITH THE MOST
FIFA World
Cup wins
BRAZIL

Brazil, host of the 2014 FIFA World Cup, has lifted the trophy the most times in the tournament's history. Second on the list, Germany, has more runners-up and semifinal appearances and hence, arguably, a stronger record overall. However, many would say that Brazil's 1970 lineup, led by the incomparable Pelé, ranks as the finest team ever. The host team has won five of the twenty tournaments that have been completed to date.

FIFA WORLD CUP WINNERS
Number of wins

Country	Wins	Years
Brazil	5	1958, 1962, 1970, 1994, 2002
Germany*	4	1954, 1974, 1990, 2014
Italy	4	1934, 1938 1982, 2006
Uruguay	2	1930, 1950
Argentina	2	1978, 1986
France	2	1998, 2018

* As West Germany 1954, 1974

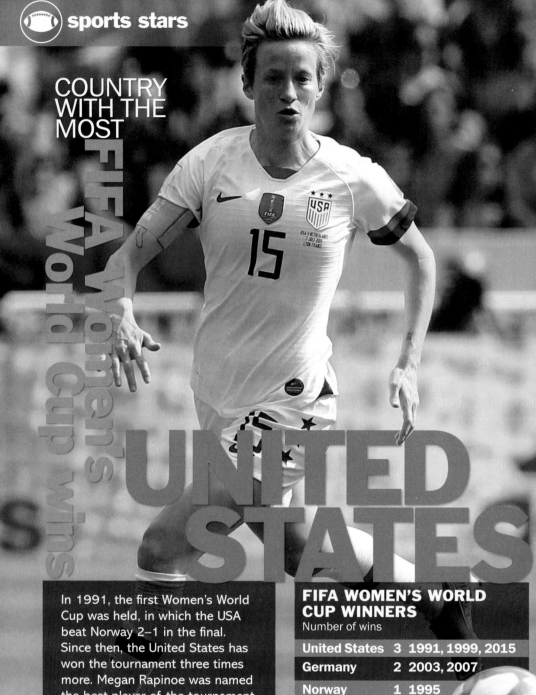

COUNTRY
WITH THE
MOST

FIFA Women's World Cup wins

UNITED STATES

In 1991, the first Women's World Cup was held, in which the USA beat Norway 2–1 in the final. Since then, the United States has won the tournament three times more. Megan Rapinoe was named the best player of the tournament following the USA's 2019 triumph. She scored the team's second goal in the 2–0 victory over the Netherlands in the final.

FIFA WOMEN'S WORLD CUP WINNERS
Number of wins

United States	3	1991, 1999, 2015
Germany	2	2003, 2007
Norway	1	1995
Japan	1	2011

KRISTINE LILLY

WOMAN WITH THE MOST international soccer caps

In her long and successful career, Kristine Lilly has played her club soccer principally with the Boston Breakers. When she made her debut on the U.S. national team in 1987, however, she was still in high school. Her total of 354 international caps is the world's highest for a man or woman and her trophy haul includes two World Cup winner's medals and two Olympic golds.

WOMEN WITH THE MOST INTERNATIONAL SOCCER CAPS
Number of caps (career years)

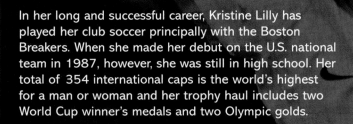

Kristine Lilly, USA	354	1987–2010
Christie Rampone, USA	311	1997–2015
Mia Hamm, USA	276	1987–2004
Julie Foudy, USA	272	1988–2004
Christine Sinclair, Canada	278	2000–

LOWEST WINNING SCORE
in a major golf tournament

In Gee Chun of South Korea is still in the early stages of her professional career but has already achieved two wins in the five annual women's golf "majors." Most remarkable of all was her achievement at the 2016 Evian Championship: the lowest score in a major championship by any player, male or female, at twenty-one under par. The previous women's record was nineteen under par, shared by five players, while two players share the men's record of twenty under par.

IN GEE CHUN

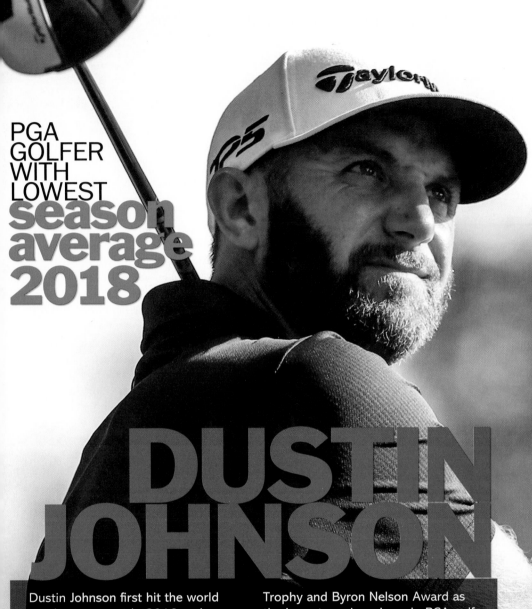

PGA GOLFER WITH LOWEST season average 2018

DUSTIN JOHNSON

Dustin Johnson first hit the world number one spot in 2016 and his current total number of weeks at number one is now fifth in the all-time rankings—and could very soon rise higher. Johnson, a South Carolinian, had a great season in 2018, taking the famous Vardon Trophy and Byron Nelson Award as the lowest scoring player in PGA golf for the second time. Johnson has so far won only one of golf's majors, the U.S. Open in 2016, but he has been particularly successful in the prestigious World Golf Championship events, with six wins to date.

WOMAN WITH THE MOST
Grand Slam titles
MARGARET
COURT

The Grand Slam tournaments are the four most important tennis events of the year: the Australian Open; the French Open; Wimbledon; and the U.S. Open. The dominant force in women's tennis throughout the 1960s and into the 1970s, Australia's Margaret Court heads the all-time singles list with twenty-four, although Serena Williams may beat this. Court won an amazing sixty-four Grand Slam titles in singles, women's doubles, and mixed doubles, a total that seems unlikely to be beaten.

TOTAL GRAND SLAM TITLES
Number of titles (singles) (years active)

Margaret Court, Australia	64 (24)	1960–1975
Martina Navratilova, Czech/USA	59 (18)	1974–2006
Serena Williams, USA	39 (23)	1998–
Billie Jean King, USA	39 (12)	1961–1980
Margaret Osborne duPont, USA	37 (6)	1941–1962

ROGER FEDERER

MAN WITH THE MOST

Grand Slam singles titles

With twenty wins, Swiss tennis star Roger Federer stands at the top of the all-time rankings in Grand Slam tennis singles tournaments. His best tournament has been Wimbledon, which he has won eight times. Federer, did not win a Grand Slam between 2012 and 2017, partly due to injury troubles. In 2017, however, after a break for knee surgery, he was back and as good as ever, with wins in Australia (repeated in 2018) and at Wimbledon.

GRAND SLAM SINGLES WINS
Number of wins (years active)

Roger Federer, Switzerland	20	1998–
Rafael Nadal, Spain	17	2001–
Novak Djokovic, Serbia	16	2003–
Pete Sampras, USA	14	1988–2002
Roy Emerson, Australia	12	1961–1973

MOST CONSECUTIVE NASCAR championship wins
JIMMIE JOHNSON

Now officially the Monster Energy NASCAR Cup Series, the NASCAR drivers' championship has been contested since 1949. California native Jimmie Johnson is tied at the top of the all-time wins list with seven, but his five-season streak, 2006–10, is easily the best in the sport's history. Johnson's racing career began on 50cc motorcycles when he was just five years old. All of Johnson's NASCAR championship wins have been achieved driving Chevrolets; his current car is a Camaro ZL1. He has won eighty-three NASCAR races so far in his career but surely has more to come.

NASCAR CHAMPIONSHIP WINS
Number of wins (years in which the title was won)

Jimmie Johnson	7 (2006, 2007, 2008, 2009, 2010, 2013, 2016)
Dale Earnhardt Sr.	7 (1980, 1986, 1987, 1990, 1991, 1993, 1994)
Richard Petty	7 (1964, 1967, 1971, 1972, 1974, 1975, 1979)
Jeff Gordon	4 (1995, 1997, 1998, 2001)

GRITTY

What's seven feet tall, bright orange, and has big eyes? It sounds like the start of a joke but since his first appearance in September 2018 Gritty, the Philadelphia Flyers' mascot, has racked up hundreds of thousands of Twitter followers. Unusually among pro sports teams, the Flyers have only had a mascot for one season before, way back in the 1970s, but in his short life Gritty has made up for this, showing up on TV talk shows and trending online. He was voted the number one mascot in the league by the NHL Players' Association in 2019.

NHL TEAM WITH THE MOST
Stanley Cup wins

The Montreal Canadiens are the oldest and, by far, the most successful National Hockey League team. In its earliest years, the Stanley Cup had various formats, but since 1927, it has been awarded exclusively to the champion NHL team—and the Canadiens have won it roughly one year in every four. Their most successful years were the 1940s through the 1970s, when the team was inspired by all-time greats like Maurice Richard and Guy Lafleur.

STANLEY CUP WINNERS (SINCE 1915)
Number of wins (time span)

Montreal Canadiens	24	1916–1993
Toronto Maple Leafs	11	1918–1967
Detroit Red Wings	11	1936–2008
Boston Bruins	6	1929–2011
Chicago Blackhawks	6	1934–2015

MONTREAL CANADIENS

NHL PLAYER WITH THE MOST
career
points

WAYNE GRETZKY

Often called "The Great One," Wayne Gretzky is regarded as the most successful hockey player. As well as scoring more goals and assists than any other NHL player—both in regular-season and in postseason games—Gretzky held over sixty NHL records in all by the time of his retirement in 1999. The majority of these records still stand. Although he was unusually small for an NHL player, Gretzky had great skills and an uncanny ability to be in the right place at the right time.

NHL ALL-TIME HIGHEST REGULAR-SEASON SCORERS
Number of points (goals) (career years)

Wayne Gretzky	2,857 (894)	1978–1999
Jaromír Jágr	1,921 (766)	1990–
Mark Messier	1,887 (694)	1979–2004
Gordie Howe	1,850 (801)	1946–1979
Ron Francis	1,798 (549)	1981–2004

 **sports stars**

CONNOR MCDAVID

At nineteen years old, center Connor McDavid was named team captain of the Edmonton Oilers at the beginning of the 2016–17 season. Remarkably, the season before that was his first in the NHL. McDavid has been hailed as the "Next One" (hockey's next household name). His value to the Oilers was made plain in 2017 when he signed a record $100 million, eight-year contract, to begin in 2018–19.

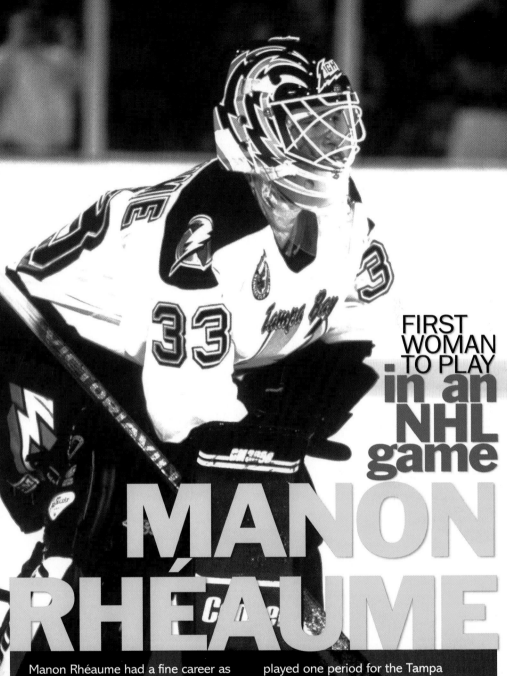

FIRST
WOMAN
TO PLAY
**in an
NHL
game**

MANON
RHÉAUME

Manon Rhéaume had a fine career as a goaltender in women's ice hockey, earning World Championship gold medals with the Canadian National Women's Team. She is also the first—and only—woman to play for an NHL club. On September 23, 1992, she played one period for the Tampa Bay Lightning in an exhibition game against the St. Louis Blues, during which she saved seven of nine shots. She later played twenty-four games for various men's teams in the professional International Hockey League.

WORLD'S LARGEST
cheerleading
cheer
HANGZHOU
CHINA

Cheerleading has a huge following around the world and is at the early stages of consideration as a possible Olympic sport. The city of Hangzhou in China staged the largest-ever cheerleading cheer in December 2018 with an astonishing 2,102 participants aged from five years old to sixty-eight. Hangzhou will be hosting the 2022 Asian Games and the event was part of the advance publicity for that championship.

MOST COMBINED-EVENT
gold medals in the Climbing World Championship

SEAN MCCOLL

Competition climbing will appear as an Olympic sport for the first time in 2020. Climbers compete on indoor climbing walls in three disciplines—lead, speed, and bouldering—to arrive at a combined score for a medal. Canada's Sean McColl has achieved three golds in the combined event (2012, 2014, 2016) at the World Championship, more than any other competitor to date. Austria's Jakob Schubert gained the 2018 title, however, and has since topped the world rankings. Slovenia's Janja Garnbret was the 2018 women's winner and is also world number one. But who will take the first-ever Olympic gold medals?

WORLD'S FASTEST
spin on ice skates
OLIVIA RYBICKA-OLIVER

Although only eleven years old at the time of her record-breaking performance, Olivia Rybicka-Oliver from Nova Scotia, Canada, achieved an astonishing spin rate of 342 revolutions per minute—over five per second. This smashed the previous record of 308 revolutions per minute.

Olivia, who is Polish by birth, set her record in Warsaw on January 19, 2015. Her performance was part of a fund-raising event held by Poland's Fundacja Dziecięca Fantazja (Children's Fantasy Foundation) for terminally ill children.

FIRST-EVER SKATER
to land six quadruple jumps

NATHAN CHEN

Nathan Chen made skating history at the 2018 Winter Olympics by being the first-ever skater to attempt and land six quadruple jumps during one performance. Quad jumps—in which the skater spins around four times while in the air—are among the hardest moves in skating, and grouping several of them in one program makes them more difficult still. Chen's record-breaking Olympic performance did not earn him a medal because he had skated poorly earlier in the competition, but a few weeks later he won the World Championship after landing his six quads once again.

MOST WINTER OLYMPICS
snowboarding gold medals
SHAUN WHITE

A professional skateboarder, successful musician, and Olympic and X-Games star, Shaun White has an astonishing range of talents. He has won more X-Games gold medals than anyone else but his three Olympic golds, in the halfpipe competitions in 2006, 2010, and 2018, the most ever by a snowboarder, are perhaps his biggest achievement. The best of all was in 2018 when he landed two super-difficult back-to-back tricks in the final round to jump into first place. White's medal happened to be the USA's 100th at the Winter Olympics; that total now stands at 105, but Norway leads in that category with 132 to date.

MOST MEDALS
won by a nation in one Summer Olympics
USA

The record medal count of 239 (including 78 golds) has been held by the United States since the 1904 Games in St. Louis, Missouri. In those days, international travel was much more difficult than it is now—as a result, it's estimated that about 90 percent of the competitors were Americans! Just twelve countries competed and only ten countries won any medals. By comparison, 206 countries competed at Rio 2016.

MOST MEDALS
won by an individual

MICHAEL PHELPS

Michael Phelps may be the greatest competitive swimmer ever. He did not win any medals at his first Olympics in 2000, but at each of the Summer Games from 2004 through 2016 he was the most successful individual athlete of any nation. When he announced his retirement after London 2012, he was already the most decorated Olympic athlete ever—but he didn't stay retired for long. At Rio 2016 he won five more golds and a silver, taking his medal total to twenty-eight—twenty-three of them gold.

MOST SUCCESSFUL OLYMPIANS
Number of medals won (gold)

Michael Phelps	USA	Swimming	2004–16	28 (23)
Larisa Latynina	USSR	Gymnastics	1956–64	18 (9)
Nikolai Andrianov	USSR	Gymnastics	1972–80	15 (7)

Four athletes, Ole Einar Bjørndalen of Norway, Boris Shakhlin of the Soviet Union, Edoardo Mangiarotti of Italy, and Takashi Ono of Japan, have each won thirteen medals.

Although she was only nineteen during the Rio Olympics, Simone Biles's four gold medals and one bronze took her medal tally from world championships and Olympics to nineteen, a new American record. Biles is only four foot eight, but her tiny frame is full of power and grace, displayed most memorably in her favorite floor exercise discipline. After a break from competing in 2017, Biles was back to her best in the 2018 World Championship, winning four golds, a silver, and a bronze. Her total of fourteen World Championship golds is also a world record.

SIMONE
BILES

Rio2016

Jamaica's Usain Bolt is the greatest track sprinter who has ever lived. Other brilliant Olympic finalists have described how all they can do is watch as he almost disappears into the distance. Usain's greatest victories have been his triple Olympic gold medals at London 2012 and Rio 2016, plus two golds from Beijing 2008. He holds the 100 meter world record (9.58s) and the 200 meter record (19.19s), both from the 2009 World Championships.

FASTEST
man in
the world
USAIN
BOLT

FASTEST 100-METER SPRINTS OF ALL TIME
Time in seconds

Usain Bolt (Jamaica) 9.58 Berlin 2009

Usain Bolt (Jamaica) 9.63 London 2012

Usain Bolt (Jamaica) 9.69 Beijing 2008

Tyson Gay (USA) 9.69 Shanghai 2009

Yohan Blake (Jamaica) 9.69 Lausanne 2012

MOST DECORATED
Paralympian ever
TRISCHA ZORN

Trischa Zorn is the most successful Paralympian of all time, having won an astonishing fifty-five medals, forty-one of them gold, at the Paralympic Games from 1980 to 2000. She won every Paralympic event she entered from 1980 to 1988. Zorn is blind and helps disabled military veterans enter the world of parasport. Zorn was inducted into the Paralympic Hall of Fame in 2012.

LEADING FEMALE PARALYMPIC MEDALISTS
Number of medals won

Trischa Zorn, USA	55
Beatrice Hess, France	25
Sarah Storey, Great Britain	25
Chantal Petitclerc, Canada	21
Mayumi Narita, Japan	20

COUNTRY WITH THE MOST
all-time Paralympic
medals
USA

Although China topped the Paralympic medal table at the 2016 Summer Games in Rio (239 medals), with the United States coming in fourth (115 medals), the United States comfortably leads the all-time medal count in the Paralympic Summer Games. Norway heads the standings in the Winter Games, with the United States in second, giving the United States an overall medal total that will be unbeatable for many years to come.

COUNTRY WITH THE MOST
PARALYMPIC MEDALS
Total number of medals won

United States	2,494
Germany*	1,871
Great Britain	1,824
Canada	1,220
France	1,209

*includes totals of former East and West Germany

FIRST
Paralympic
triathlon
RIO 2016

Most people would find a 750-meter swim, followed by a 20-kilometer bike ride, then a 5-kilometer run quite challenging—but then try all that with a physical or visual impairment, too. That's how it is for paratriathletes. Sixty Paralympians qualified for the first-ever Olympic paratriathlon at Rio in 2016. Only six of the possible ten events (men and women) were contested in Rio, with the United States' two golds, one silver, and one bronze being the best national result.

Photo credits

Dreamstime; 182-183: Stephen Alvarez/National Geographic Image Collection; 184: De Beers Group; 185: Nguyen-Anh Le/Getty Images; 186 top: Robert Adrian Hillman/Shutterstock; 186 background: ibrandify gallery/Shutterstock; 187: Pete Atkinson/Getty Images; 188: Guilu/Dreamstime; 188: Valentin Armianu/Dreamstime; 189: Jeff Schmaltz, MODIS Rapid Response Team/NASA; 190: Imagineimages/Dreamstime; 191: stellaristock/iStockphoto; 192 top left: Keitma/Alamy Stock Photo; 192 bottom left: Gerald Herbert/AP Images; 193 top: Kelly Barnes/EPA-EFE/Shutterstock; 193 center: Miguel Candela/SOPA Images/Shutterstock; 193 bottom: Ayhan Mehmet/Getty Images; 194: Dean Conger/Getty Images; 195: Daniel Kreher/age fotostock; 196-197: APFootage/Alamy Stock Photo; 198: Tigeryan/iStockphoto; 199: eyecrave/iStockphoto; 200: Michele Cornelius/Dreamstime; 201: Everett Collection/age fotostock; 202: Imaginechina/AP Images; 203: CampPhoto/iStockphoto; 204: Nadine Spires/Dreamstime; 205: Dark Moon Pictures/Shutterstock; 206-207: Jeff Bukowski/Shutterstock; 208 top: Michael Reynolds/EPA-EFE/Shutterstock; 208 bottom: Shawn Thew/EPA-EFE/Shutterstock; 209 top right: Andrey_Popov/Shutterstock; 209 top right inset: Vitalii Smulskyi/Shutterstock; 209 center: Steven Ferdman/Shutterstock; 209 bottom right: Beyond Meat; 210: Dan Anderson via ZUMA Wire/Newscom; 211: Alaska Stock/age fotostock; 211 icons: Walking-onstreet/Shutterstock; 212: Russ Kinne/age fotostock; 213: PODIS/Shutterstock; 213 diamonds: Gems Collection/Shutterstock; 214: Sam Gangwer/The Orange County Register/ZUMAPRESS.com/Newscom; 215: aznature/Thinkstock; 216: Randy Duchaine/Alamy Stock Photo; 217: Newman Mark/age fotostock; 218: Lequint/Dreamstime; 219: Anneka/Shutterstock; 220: Lucy Pemoni/AP Images; 221: Steve Conner/Getty Images; 222: Nagel Photography/Shutterstock; 223: Buyenlarge/Getty Images; 224: Don Smetzer/Alamy Stock Photo; 225: Keith Kapple/SuperStock, Inc.; 226: Stephen J. Cohen/Getty Images; 227: John Cancalosi/Pantheon/SuperStock, Inc.; 228: johnwoodcock/iStockphoto; 229: Dave Newman/Shutterstock; 230: Ramona Kaulitzki/Shutterstock; 231: Orange Vectors/Shutterstock; 231 icons: a Sk/Shutterstock; 232: Jeff Bukowski/Shutterstock; 233: Richard Finkelstein for USA IBC; 234: Historic Collection/Alamy Stock Photo; 235: Edgloris E. Marys/age fotostock; 236: Robert_Ford/iStockphoto; 237: Bob Thomason/Getty Images; 238: Nansen Ski Club; 239: Loop Images/Getty Images; 240 sky: detchana wangkheeree/Shutterstock; 240 bottom: Visit Las Cruces; 241: RoadsideAmerica.com; 242: Alan Marler/AP Images; 243: StudioSmart/Shutterstock; 244: Library of Congress; 245: John Elk III/Getty Images; 246: Stas Moroz/Shutterstock; 247: Matt Rourke/AP Images; 248: Jerry Coli/Dreamstime; 249: Ed Currie/PuckerButt Pepper Company; 250: Sergio Pitamitz/age fotostock; 251 center: Louella938/Shutterstock; 251 background: Christophe Boisson/Shutterstock; 252: Patrick Byrd/Getty Images; 253: Johnny Adolphson/Dreamstime; 254: Tara Golden/Dreamstime; 255: Frontpage/Shutterstock; 256: Kevin Schafer/Getty Images; 257: Jon Bilous/Shutterstock; 258: Tom Lynn/Getty Images; 259: Richard Maschmeyer/age fotostock; 260-261: IPS/Shutterstock; 262 top: Jayne Kamin-Oncea/Getty Images; 262 bottom: Chris Allan/Shutterstock; 263 top: Ian Walton/Shutterstock; 263 bottom left: Fazry Ismail/EPA-EFE/Shutterstock; 263 bottom right: John Cordes/AP Images; 264: ZJAN/Supplied by WENN.com/Newscom; 265: Gian Ehrenzeller/EPA/Shutterstock; 266: Streeter Lecka/Getty Images; 267: Associated Press/AP Images; 268: HowRidiculous.org; 269: Chris Sweda/Getty Images; 270: Focus on Sport/Getty Images; 271: Mark J. Terrill/AP Images; 272: Barry Gossage/Getty Images; 273: Tom Szczerbowski/Getty Images; 274: Greg Trott/AP Images; 275: Dave Shopland/BPI/Shutterstock; 276: IPS/Shutterstock; 277: Kevork Djansezian/Getty Images; 278: Jed Jacobsohn/Getty Images; 279: Jamie Squire/Getty Images; 280: Mark Rucker/Getty Images; 281: Denis Poroy/AP Images; 282: Victor Decolongon/Getty Images; 283 tape: clsgraphics/iStockphoto; 283: Associated Press/AP Images; 284: David Vincent/AP/Shutterstock; 285: Guang Niu/Getty Images; 286: Chatchai Somwat/Dreamstime; 287: Shawn Thew/EPA-EFE/Shutterstock; 288: Daily Express/Getty Images; 289: Anja Niedringhaus/AP Images; 290: Jared C. Tilton/Getty Images; 291: Bruce Bennett/Getty Images; 292: Ryan Remiorz/AP Images; 293: Rocky Widner/Getty Images; 294: Minas Panagiotakis/Getty Images; 295: Al Messerschmidt/AP Images; 296: mhodges/iStockphoto; 297: Miguel Medina/GettyImages; 298: David Madison/Getty Images; 299: Marco Bertorello/Getty Images; 300: The Yomiuri Shimbun/AP Images; 301: Popperfoto/Getty Images; 302: Mitchell Gunn/Dreamstime; 303: Zhukovsky/Dreamstime; 304: David Phillip/AP Images; 305: Aris Messinis/Getty Images; 306: Raphael Dias/Getty Images; 307: Buda Mendes/Getty Images.

SCHOLASTIC SUMMER
READ-A-PALOOZA
READ · CELEBRATE · GIVE

The 2019 Scholastic Read-a-Palooza Summer Reading Challenge was one for the books! For 18 weeks this summer, Scholastic encouraged kids to read every day. Those minutes added up quickly and helped make a BIG difference! By reading a total of **109,334,297** minutes, kids helped to unlock a donation of **200,000 books** from Scholastic. The books were distributed to kids with limited or no access to books through United Way locations across the country! (P.S. - This is the seventh year in a row kids read more than 100 million minutes!)

CONGRATULATIONS TO EVERYONE
WHO PARTICIPATED IN 2019!

TOP 20 STATES WITH THE MOST MINUTES READ

DID YOU MAKE THE TOP 20?

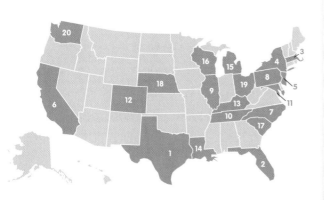

Number of participating schools: **1,737**
Number of schools logging 100,000 minutes or more: **215**

1. Texas	11,499,116
2. Florida	9,709,187
3. Massachusetts	8,121,898
4. New York	7,628,437
5. New Jersey	5,729,363
6. California	5,553,335
7. North Carolina	4,740,291
8. Pennsylvania	4,320,375
9. Illinois	2,776,081
10. Tennessee	2,583,152
11. Maryland	2,491,913
12. Colorado	2,145,857
13. Kentucky	2,074,950
14. Louisiana	2,046,200
15. Michigan	1,974,366
16. Wisconsin	1,894,184
17. South Carolina	1,776,567
18. Nebraska	1,726,781
19. Ohio	1,615,247
20. Washington	1,507,539

TOP LIBRARIES & COMMUNITY PARTNERS	CITY & STATE
Dustin Michael Sekula Memorial Library	Edinburg, TX
Pickford Community Library	Pickford, MI
Albia Public Library	Albia, IA
Okeechobee County Library	Okeechobee, FL
Choteau/Teton Public Library	Choteau, MT
Gibbon Public Library	Gibbon, NE
Community Progress Council Home Base Program	York, PA
Girl Scouts Troop 2241	Turlock, CA
Moravia Public Library	Moravia, IA
Joseph H. Plumb Memorial Library	Rochester, MA

HONORABLE MENTIONS! STUDENTS AT THESE SCHOOLS REACHED THIS AWESOME MILESTONE!

MILLION MINUTE READERS CLUB!	CITY & STATE
Mitchell Intermediate School	The Woodlands, TX
New River Elementary School	Wesley Chapel, FL
Parkland Middle School	El Paso, TX
Daley Middle School	Lowell, MA
Hirsch Elementary School	Freemont, CA

These are the results as of 9/14 for the Summer Reading Challenge. To find out more, please visit *scholastic.com/summer*.

STATE	SCHOOL	CITY
Alabama	Mt. Carmel Elementary	Huntsville
Alaska	North Pole Elementary School	North Pole
Arizona	American Leadership Academy - Ironwood Elementary	Queen Creek
Arkansas	The New School	Fayetteville
California	Warm Springs Elementary School	Fremont
Colorado	Prospect Ridge Academy	Broomfield
Connecticut	Scotland Elementary School	Scotland
Delaware	Etta J. Wilson Elementary School	Newark
District of Columbia	Holy Trinity School	Washington, DC
Florida	Liberty Park Elementary School	Greenacres
Georgia	Savannah Country Day School	Savannah
Hawaii	Kanoelani Elementary School	Waipahu
Idaho	Compass Public Charter School	Meridian
Illinois	Walnut Trails Elementary School	Shorewood
Indiana	Allisonville Elementary School	Indianapolis
Iowa	Clayton Ridge Elementary School	Guttenberg
Kansas	St. Thomas Aquinas School	Wichita
Kentucky	Veterans Park Elementary	Lexington
Louisiana	Lisa Park Elementary School	Houma
Maine	Buxton Center Elementary School	Buxton
Maryland	Bradley Hills Elementary School	Bethesda
Massachusetts	James M. Quinn Elementary School	North Dartmouth
Michigan	St. Clair Middle School	St. Clair
Minnesota	Maranatha Christian Academy	Brooklyn Park
Mississippi	Annunciation Catholic School	Columbus
Missouri	Murphy Elementary School	High Ridge
Montana	Bonner K-8 School	Bonner
Nebraska	Stuart Elementary School	Stuart
Nevada	Jan Jones Blackhurst Elementary School	Las Vegas
New Hampshire	Rochester Middle School	Rochester
New Jersey	Newell Elementary School	Allentown
New Mexico	Chamisa Elementary	White Rock
New York	Village Elementary School	Hilton
North Carolina	A.B. Combs Leadership Magnet Elementary School	Raleigh
North Dakota	Erik Ramstad Middle School	Minot
Northern Mariana Islands	Saipan Community School	Saipan
Ohio	Ledgeview Elementary School	Macedonia
Oklahoma	Colcord Public School	Colcord
Oregon	Holy Cross Catholic School	Portland
Pennsylvania	Skippack Elementary School	Collegeville
Puerto Rico	Robinson School	San Juan
Rhode Island	North Smithfield Elementary School	North Smithfield
South Carolina	Oakridge Elementary School	Clover
South Dakota	Aberdeen Christian School	Aberdeen
Tennessee	Crosswind Elementary School	Collierville
Texas	Eastwood Knolls International School	El Paso
US Virgin Islands	Joseph Gomez Elementary School	St. Thomas
Utah	Freedom Academy	Provo
Vermont	Orwell Village School	Orwell
Virginia	Ashburn Elementary School	Ashburn
Washington	Sunrise Elementary School	Spokane Valley
West Virginia	St. Francis Central Catholic School	Morgantown
Wisconsin	Riverdale Elementary-Middle School	Muscoda
Wyoming	Casper Classical Academy	Casper

SCHOLASTIC SUMMER READ-A-PALOOZA

READ · CELEBRATE · GIVE

GIVING BACK BY READING

The Scholastic Read-a-Palooza Summer Reading Give Back empowered kids to increase book access for other kids in two ways: by donating books at local Summer Reading Celebrations, and by entering their reading minutes in the Summer Reading Challenge, helping to unlock book donations from Scholastic and United Way.

At the Florida Department of Health and DeSoto School District's Back to School Fair, United Way Suncoast distributed school supplies from local community partners as well as free books from Scholastic as part of the Read-a-Palooza Summer Reading Give Back! (Photo via @UWSuncoast/Twitter)

In Texas, at the Community Development Corporation of Brownsville's Back to School Block Party, the United Way of Southern Cameron County distributed free Scholastic Read-a-Palooza Summer Reading Give Back titles to local families! (Photo via United Way of Southern Cameron County/Facebook)

Milwaukee, Wisconsin's Boswell Book Company welcomed Clifford the Big Red Dog to their Read-a-Palooza Summer Reading Celebration! They collected books for Next Door, an early childhood organization that focuses on improving literacy and school readiness for children ages 0–5 in Milwaukee's central city. (Photo via @NextDoorMil/Twitter)

As part of their Read-a-Palooza Summer Reading Celebration, University Book Store in Seattle, Washington, collected donations for the Northwest Literacy Foundation, which works to enhance youth literacy in the Pacific Northwest by providing literature and resources to underserved communities. (Photo via @ubookstoresea/Twitter)

SCHOLASTIC SUMMER
READ-A-PALOOZA
READ · CELEBRATE · GIVE

SUMMER READING CHALLENGE HIGHLIGHTS

Reaching minute milestones, celebrating reading achievements, and curling up with a good book (and a very good dog) — here are some highlights from the Scholastic Read-a-Palooza Summer Reading Challenge!

Way to go! Students from A.B. Combs Leadership Magnet Elementary School in North Carolina read 1,217,593 million minutes in their fifth year of participating in the Scholastic Read-a-Palooza Summer Reading Challenge! School librarians encouraged kids to read all summer long by hosting a kickoff assembly when the Challenge began in May, and by posting a "leader board" highlighting top readers. (Photo via A.B. Combs Leadership Magnet Elementary School)

We shared our excitement on social media when we reached major summer reading minute milestones: 25, 50, and 100 million minutes!

Summer reading is even better with a (furry) friend! (Photo via @jmalphy/Twitter)

Students at Eastwood Knolls International School in El Paso, Texas, read over three million minutes this summer! Congratulations to these readers on their Texas-sized achievement! (Photo via Eastwood Knolls International School)